THE UNSTOPPABLE EVENTREPRENEUR™

TURNING YOUR **PASSION** FOR EVENTS
INTO YOUR **PROFITABLE** BUSINESS

MAY YEO SILVERS

A MULTIPLE 6 FIGURE EVENTREPRENEUR, FOUNDER
& OWNER OF M2 HOSPITALITY & EVENTS4ANYONE

Disclaimer: Eventrepreneur is a word that was created by May Yeo Silvers and cannot be found in the dictionary.
EVENTrepreneur™ is trademarked by May Yeo Silvers

Edited by Susan K. Csomor

An Imprint for GracePoint Publishing (www.GracePointPublishing.com)

GracePoint Matrix, LLC
624 S. Cascade Ave, Suite 201, Colorado Springs, CO 80903
www.GracePointMatrix.com
Email: Admin@GracePointMatrix.com
SAN # 991-6032

Library of Congress Control Number: 2023942547

ISBN: (Paperback) 978-1-955272-26-1
ISBN: (Hardcover) 978-1-961347-10-6
eISBN: 978-1-955272-27-8

Books may be purchased for educational, business, or sales promotional use.
For bulk order requests and price schedule contact:
Orders@GracePointPublishing.com

I dedicate this book to my daughter Mia, for showing me how to be a better human and leader, and to my husband Matt, for loving me for who I am.

TABLE OF CONTENTS

WHAT IS AN UNSTOPPABLE EVENTREPRENEUR™?

An Unstoppable Eventrepreneur is a person who is going all in and turning their passion for planning events into a profitable business. They equip themselves with the necessary business skills to grow and scale their business, not losing sight of their WHY. An Unstoppable Eventrepreneur has a clear vision of why they do what they do. They form a synergy of doing what they love, planning events, and seeing the delight in their clients' faces, and creating a profitable business at the same time.

An Unstoppable Eventrepreneur has great visions, is creative and extremely resourceful. An Unstoppable Eventrepreneur's whole purpose is to articulate their client's vision—the maestro conducting the symphony of managing all the vendors where everyone plays a role to bring the vision into reality. While an Unstoppable Eventrepreneur is making visions of events come true, they are also the CEO of their event planning business, being a leader in the events field, educating and inspiring their team, their partners in the events field, and also their clients.

So, are you ready to become an Unstoppable Eventrepreneur?

INTRODUCTION

Greetings Eventrepreneurs! What you are holding in your hands, or reading on your screen, thanks to the vast technology of our modern world, is the best, most condensed resource for understanding what it takes to create a thriving, successful six-figure event planning business. I created this book to support your event-repreneur journey in the best way possible, hopefully helping you to avoid some of the same mistakes I made and have seen others make time and time again prior to them joining our Unstoppable EVENTrepreneur Mentorship Program™.

Is event planning an easy business venture to start and to scale? Yes, it certainly is—IF you know what you are doing. It does not have to be as difficult as we can sometimes make it for ourselves. I am here to support and show you some great ways to learn how to make the path of eventrepreneurship easier.

To begin, I share a lot of my own personal journey with you in this book. It has been a labor of love, much like anything else I undertake. I have tried to organize it in a way that is easy to access and to understand. First and foremost, I give a broad overview of how the book is organized by chapter, in case you need to access a specific area at any given time while you are building your business. I hope you find exactly what you need within my book's pages to give you the confidence and knowledge to create the life of your dreams by doing what you love—planning events!

Chapter One describes my story. This encompasses my background, education, and career journey, to include beginning a business with two leads, no pipeline for work, and then having to go back out into the corporate world as an employee, for financial security/fear of no income.

The birth of my child eventually propelled me into the mindset necessary to build my event planning business and became my Why. As a result, I am able to share my story with the world to provide advice and guidance for other small business owners, specifically eventrepreneurs.

Chapter Two contains my mission statement. I discuss my experience, my credentials, and present myself as your consultant, counselor, and cheerleader. This chapter helps set up the idea that everyone comes to entrepreneurship through their own path, their own journey. Like a jigsaw puzzle, the book will help readers begin to put together their own individualized plan for success which includes creating opportunities, learning from others, and knowing and understanding their Why. Readers will begin to understand how to turn their Why into a profitable event planning business.

Chapter Three helps explain what qualities contribute to being a Successful Event Planner AND an Unstoppable EVENTrepreneur. This chapter speaks to the idea that all event planners have their own Zone of Genius, and all event planners can be great in their own ways. This makes it imperative that each eventrepreneur knows their passion and their superpower. It describes the importance of being organized, planner/client relationships, productivity, how you spend your energy, alignment, and all of the practical considerations for a successful, six-figure event planning business. These include contracts, marketing, social media, partnership with venues and vendors.

Chapter Four discusses the important steps in figuring out what kind of event planner you want to be. This chapter asks readers some important questions around what kind of events they like planning and what their signature style will be, as key to helping them figure out how to be sure they are reaching their target audience of ideal clients. I encourage eventrepreneurs to interview themselves and figure out why they are the best at what they do, in their field. This keeps event planners from spreading themselves across too many areas and helps them to discern the difference between event planners and event designers.

Chapter Five instructs on the absolute imperative piece of knowing and assessing your own financial structure and stability. This chapter gets gritty on the details of evaluating where you are financially at all stages of your business. It advises how to get comfortable with knowing all of your financial details, even if it is your tendency to be uncomfortable with money and numbers. It speaks to the do's and don'ts of partnering in business, vendor contracts, and the ever-sensitive topic of how to price the services you provide, and how and when to raise them accordingly. This chapter also addresses good ways to discuss your clients' budgets, as well as ways to handle any cost objections.

Chapter Six sets a clear description of what you need and what you don't need to start your event planning business. Containing tangible as well as intangible elements, it is a practical, quick reference list of information that condenses some of my best advice into one place.

Chapter Seven, simply put, explains some of the common pitfalls that can occur when an eventrepreneur chooses to open their business, and even along the way as the business grows. These pitfalls can happen at any business level to anyone who strives to be something greater or strives to grow their business to that six-figure level and beyond. Self-doubt does not discriminate by any means or category. This chapter acknowledges the growing pains felt by most business owners at one time or another.

As a part of the growing pains, Chapter Eight reframes the inner conversation most of us have had with fear and how to relate to your fears in a new way. All entrepreneurs face and feel fear of the unknown, what sets successful eventrepreneurs apart is how they manage and respond to those fears. Competition is included in this chapter as a potential fear, and I explain that if there was no competition for your services, there would be no market potential for what you are trying to sell.

Chapter Nine speaks to the differences between a CEO Mindset and an Employee Mindset. This chapter helps eventrepreneurs identify their habitual patterns of behavior and how to evolve beyond their old ways of doing things. Whether moving your business from new to seasoned, or side-hustle to main-job, the process of leveling up provides opportunities to examine your schedule and make appropriate adjustments to handle the responsibilities of being a CEO, which grow in scope as the business grows.

Chapter Ten contains my final thoughts on growing your business and best wishes for the health and success of your business. Closing the book, I leave the reader with some inspiration for achievable goals and how you can absorb all the learning in the world, but without application, there is no translation into your life and your business. I offer you my continued and extended assistance and ways to keep in touch with me on the different Unstoppable Event-repreneur platforms.

TEN ROOKIE MISTAKES

A Note About Rookie Mistakes:

Before we begin! Potentially unpopular opinion: Some of the best teachers we have are the mistakes we make.

It's just true. We don't know what we don't know, until we know it! It's okay, you now have your resource to prevent the perpetuation of what I like to call "Rookie Mistakes." The following is a list of Eventrepreneur Rookie Mistakes that I have seen and experienced throughout my event-repreneurship journey.

TEN ROOKIE MISTAKES

1. Buying inventory.

You are an event planner, you want to own an event planning business, right? Unless you plan to be in the event decor/prop/furniture rental business, why do you need inventory? As an event planner, you form relationships with vendors, like event decor/prop/furniture rental companies, so you can rent from them at an industry rate. They keep up with the maintenance of the inventory and the latest trends in the events industry, and they also have the space to store this inventory. Do you want your home or your garage to become a storage space??

2. Investing in office space.

One of the perks of being an event planner is that we have the flexibility to work anywhere in the world as long as we have our laptop and internet. Why do you want to have an office? To show that you are a legit business? You are legit when you register your company with the state. You are legit when you have paying clients. Having an office doesn't make you legit. It may make you FEEL legit, but that's ego and insecurity talking. If you say you want your clients to come to your office for meetings, sorry to break this to you honey, YOU go to your client. You meet your client wherever they are. Now that we are able to use virtual meeting options, who needs an office???

3. Not understanding your financials.

If you decide to just quit your job and go all in into your event planning business, you have got guts, kudos to you. If your risk appetite is high, this may be the best decision you will ever make. If you thrive in a "do or die" situation, you will rise to the occasion and bust your tooshie to make it happen.

However, if your risk appetite is low, and you don't function well under the pressure of not knowing when the next paycheck is, you MUST know your financials before you decide to ditch your day job to go work full time for your business. If you don't assess your financial risk appetite and understand your financials, I am almost certain that you will go BACK to look for a full-time job the very first time you see your account running low and start to worry about not having enough money in your bank account to pay your bills.

4. Spending your own money on client's events.

You want the events you planned to look beautiful, but your client only gave you a small budget to pull off the event. Because you are so passionate about what you do, and you have so much pride for your work, you forked out YOUR OWN MONEY to make the event look good. You just turned your passion into an expensive hobby.

5. Bidding too low.

You want that client, the competition is stiff, and you are so afraid of losing the client that you go into a price bidding war so you can get the client. You win this bidding war! What happens when you do that? You build yourself a reputation that you are the "cheap" event planner and start getting "cheap" clients. Unfortunately, this leads to you continuing to do your work at a "cheap" price, and you eventually realize that you worked your butt off for pennies, if any money at all. You start to resent what you do, and your passion fizzles. Do you need me to elaborate more?

6. Thinking that if you build it, they will come.

How could your clients come to you when they don't even know you exist? Your ego tells you that you do great work, but how would you expect anyone to know that your work is great when you make no effort to broadcast your work??

Rule number one in business: Always sell and market what you offer. Rule number 2: Refer to rule number one. Remember, if they can't find you, they can't pay you.

7. Waiting for perfection (getting ducks in a row).

Sorry to burst your perfectionist bubble, you will never get your ducks in a row. In business, the mother goose is ALWAYS chasing the ducklings. When you think you have one thing down pat, something else will require your attention. There is NEVER an ideal time to start a business or to take any actions to work on your business. The motto in business is to take action, even if it isn't perfect, be obsessed with progression, not perfection.

8. Comparing your day one to other people's day one hundred.

Why would you do that? That's the number one sabotage to yourself and your business. You know who is the biggest and only competitor? Look in the mirror. YOU are the biggest competitor. You should compare YOUR day one hundred to your day one, not someone else's. You have no idea what resources they have access to and how they operate. All you see is the surface. There are many planners out there who say they have a "business," and in reality, they have a company name and website, that's it. As long as you have progressed from your day one to day one hundred, that's what matters.

9. Feeling paralyzed with "I don't know how to do this."

If you want to be an Unstoppable Eventrepreneur, you better learn how to complete that sentence, "I don't know how to do this, BUT I will figure it out."

Feeling paralyzed is not going to get you anywhere. There is always a solution to a problem/challenge. The question is, are you making the choice to research and receive the solution and take action?

10. Being afraid to ask for the business.

You want to make money for your business? If your answer is yes, why are you afraid to ask for it? The money is yours, all you have to do is to CLAIM it!

You are afraid to ask for the business because you are afraid that you will get a NO. You are afraid of rejection.

A sale is a business transaction where money is exchanged for a service. A client happily and willingly hands you her money, and you happily and confidently accept her money in exchange for your service.

If a potential client does not feel that you can provide the service you say you can provide, the sale won't happen. The potential client is not rejecting YOU, don't take it personally. They are just rejecting what you are offering because maybe what you are offering is not exactly what they are looking for.

BUT if your potential client feels that you are the event planner for her, AND you don't ask for the sale, they don't know what else is expected of them since they already expressed they want to work with you. Don't ever put your potential client in a situation where they need to figure out what to do next. ASK FOR THE SALE, and the clients will happily hand the money over to you.

Do you recognize any of these in yourself or in any of the other event planners you know or work with? If the answer is "Yes," this book is PERFECT for you, read on to find out why…

CHAPTER 1

MY STORY

It is one hundred percent possible to do what you love and be well compensated for it to live the life that you want and to, in turn, give the "good life" to your loved ones. My journey to being an Unstoppable Eventrepreneur has taken many turns. It has landed me in a place where I am happy, business is growing, and I love what I do. I love what I do so much that I am now at a point where I want to share my journey with you in the hope that my experience in a highly competitive industry can help you create a successful event planning business of your own.

Eventrepreneurship came to me after I realized I had the skills and drive to take what I learned in my studies and combine it with my hands-on work experience to create a multi-six-figure business. I worked in the hospitality field for sixteen years specializing in catering sales, conference services, and food and beverage. However, it wasn't a linear process nor an easy one.

Successful business management does not come easy to all people, even if they study it.

Initially, I studied Tourism Management in Singapore and furthered my studies in Switzerland at Glion Institute of Higher Education, majoring in Hospitality Administration.

I began working in hospitality in the hotel industry. I learned a lot, but, if I hadn't gotten to know the right people at the right time, in the right place, with the right attitude AND a great mentor, I would never be where I am today.

When I was given the food and beverage (F&B) management trainee position at the Raffles Hotel in Singapore after I graduated in 1996, I took a look at what HR had planned for me and I said, "No way." Six months in the same restaurant as a server? I don't need six months to learn how to serve.

I asked to change the training schedule. I made sure the food and beverage director knew who I was and showed him how eager I was to learn EVERYTHING about food and beverage. I also demonstrated how hard I would work to learn whatever he wanted to teach me.

So, he did end up changing my training schedule because I was the only F&B trainee who spoke up about what I wanted. I learned so much because of the opportunity he had given me, but more importantly, I took advantage of that opportunity and made something out of it. I was tenacious, hungry for opportunities, and ready to learn. No task was too low or dirty, and I was not afraid to speak up as I crafted my own path. I was laser focused.

While I was working hard, I also made sure I was enjoying the learning journey. I had so much passion for what I was doing that I felt little exhaustion. I still recall one night I was assigned to the stewarding department, and we had an Indian wedding. I washed so many dishes my hands smelled like curry for the next few days, but I paid attention to the structure of the event, the details, and I learned.

I could never thank this man enough. The godfather of F&B at the famous grand dame, the Raffles Hotel of Singapore. After I finished my overseas education and returned to Singapore to work in the hotel industry, this same man gave me a call eight years later and asked if I would come to the United States and help him do a hotel opening in South Beach, Miami, Florida. This changed my life forever.

I believe the moral of my story is that a good education is JUST the foundation, but it won't get you anywhere if you don't have the right attitude and assert yourself in the right environment.

One of the greatest adversaries to successful business ownership is fear. We discuss this later in the book in Chapter Eight, but my journey to successful eventrepreneurship would not be complete without a description of how fear greatly affected my life for a time and catapulted me into creating my successful, six-figure event planning business. I accepted the fear for what it was and changed my relationship to it.

At the very beginning of my event planning business, I remember I had secured two clients. It was great! However, when those two jobs were over, I didn't have a clear plan for how to market myself and reach out for more clients. I thought that it was a fluke that I got the first two clients. I didn't even know how I got those two clients. If I don't really know what I am doing, how am I going to pay my bills if it was just a fluke?

It was scary! So, I ended up going back to my financial comfort zone working for someone else. Even though I had previously been able to reach my goal of making $100,000, it was done working for other people. Owning my own business made it very daunting that now I had to go find that hundred thousand dollars by myself.

Going back to work for someone else, I was able to just show up to work and didn't have to worry about it. I never put together that the same principle would have worked for my own event planning business as well: All I needed to do for my business was to show up and work on my business. Looking back, it seems very simple now.

In the hotel business, I was in a good position. I knew I would be able to achieve my financial goals and be able to pay my bills through earning my $100,000. So, I never thought that the other, eventrepreneur, way of thinking was to show up for my business, and I would make $200,000-$300,000.

I think it's a very common entrepreneurial fear to go back to what we know. Then, you tell yourself that once you're financially stable, if your business is not making money, it's okay because you still have money coming in. It's a slippery slope because then, you start treating your business as a scant side hustle, and if you start treating your business as a really, really tiny side hustle, it will remain a tiny side hustle. It will never become your full-time job.

So, that's what I did, for one year and three months, I had a job working for other people. I quit the first job because my boss was terrible, which reminded me why I wanted to work for myself in the first place. After I quit the first job, the money was so good, I immediately went out and got another job.

I hadn't gotten out of the fear. I began to ask myself, how many times do you need to be slapped in the face, but I still took the job. When I took the job, I was still working on the business, but I wasn't growing my business. I was just working on the remnants of my existing clients.

I began to compromise what I wanted financially in order to continue to have what I call perceived financial security. Even though it was less than what I wanted to earn, the idea of being employed full-time took precedence as representation of stability.

I took a job that paid a lower salary plus commission. With commission, I was able to earn about $80,000, and I told myself, "It's okay. A $20,000 loss is better than the potential of not making any money if I were to run my own business." I was still living in the perceived safety of an income that came from working for someone else.

I was a great employee. I made my employer a lot of money, to the tune of millions of dollars. In addition, I had created ten to twelve new accounts on my employer's behalf. Even though I was doing so well at my job, I was struggling internally as I had in the past because I have the same challenge everywhere I work. I always ended up feeling that there was a better way to run a business. Not only was there a better way to run a business, but there was also a better way to treat employees, even though the person that I went to work for this time around was a dear friend of mine. He knew how I felt.

It was at this time that I got married, and then I got pregnant, and he said to me, "When you see the face of your baby, you will never want to come back and work for other people. You will want to spend as much time with your child as you possibly can." He was right.

When I saw my sweet baby's face, I knew that was it. It was do or die. I spoke to my husband, and him being my pillar was extremely important, which is why I now advise that when you start your business, you must make sure that you have a very supportive and entrepreneurially conducive environment. If your family doesn't support you, they also shouldn't stop you. They don't have to be 200% on board, but they also don't need to be the ones who stand in your way of trying your very best to build your dream career, and therefore, life. This time was the tipping point for me.

When I had my daughter, I had no business. My accounts had all dried up, so I started thinking, what do I need to do to make this happen? Even though my husband is my pillar, I mention in later chapters that I was taught never to depend on anyone for my financial freedom and well-being. So, I would work when I had time. Sometimes it was 1:00 a.m., and I was making connections online. Sometimes it was 4:00 a.m., and I would pump breast milk while sending out emails for appointments with vendors and for meeting potential clients.

I remember I had a portable breast pump machine that I would use while I was driving from appointment to appointment. Often, I would feed the baby, and then go back out for the rest of my meetings. Sometimes I had to pump in the bathroom at the meeting sites. I would time my appointments with a four-hour gap, so I could conduct my meetings, and make it home while my daughter was just about to wake up.

I was willing to do whatever it took to make my business successful, giving me the financial stability to not only pay my bills, but live a beautiful life with my family, working only the hours that I set for myself.

In the beginning, it was challenging, but oh, it has been so worth the effort, and now I am able to share with you ways that can support you to build your own successful, six-figure event planning business.

CHAPTER 2

MY MISSION STATEMENT

When I left my lucrative full-time job in the hospitality industry to start my event planning business, some people told me I was crazy to leave a cushy job. Others commented on my "bravery" to leave the corporate world, especially when I was working with luxury hotel chains holding a senior management position.

Several of my close acquaintances were envious and admired my commitment to create the life that I wanted to live while doing what I love. Fast forward nine years. After establishing M2 Hospitality, my event planning company, into a multiple six figure business and with the occurrence of Covid causing several of my friends in the hospitality industry to lose their jobs, I felt a calling to start a business coaching program for event planners AND to write a book. My purpose is to share my journey on how I built my business, and this will hopefully inspire more event planners to be an active participant in their life instead of a spectator, take charge, and start making decisions that will lead them to live their best life.

Having an established business is not a requirement for benefitting from the information you will find here. This book is for ALL of you! We are eventrepreneurs at any and every stage of our business building.

With over twenty years of experience in the events field while writing this book, I have been able to identify and name some guiding principles in this business that will support you at whatever stage you find yourself. It is my goal to help support you in reaching YOUR goals. I will talk about various topics that appeal to a broad audience. I will be talking to people who are considering if the hospitality and events industry is a career for them, novice event planners who want to get some event planning tips, and professional event planners who want to gather resources from event industry leaders.

Along the way, I will quote real-life examples using my own hospitality career journey and as the owner of an event planning company. Consider me your consultant, counselor, and cheerleader.

There are no income requirements or success benchmarks necessary to use the information provided here. In terms of potential revenue as an eventrepreneur, the range of earning is vast. An event planner just beginning can earn on average $10,000 per year, and for an experienced planner with a steady database of clients, it is not uncommon to make between $250,000 to $500,000.

To reach income of that level, you don't have to own inventory, decorations, or go right out and find a space to rent to physically house your business. In fact, I wholeheartedly advise against that. Building a team and subcontracting become pivotal to success.

When I started, I was smart enough not to own any inventory. I STILL don't own inventory in my event planning business. It is still just me in my company, working with a lot of contractors and vendors who I consider my team.

I am not saying this is the only way to work in this business. This is not the only path; it's just my path, and I share my experiences with you to help you make the best choices for you and your eventrepreneur business. I started with nothing. You don't always have to ascribe to the jump-in-with-both-feet school of thought. It is not for everybody. It depends on your risk appetite and risk tolerance.

Assess your risk appetite and your financial safety net. My business was a side-hustle first, mostly because of financial fears, before I took the plunge to dedicate all my work energy to building and growing M2 Hospitality. Within two years, because of my passion for creating beautiful, well-planned events for my clients, I had increased my income to over $100,000, working MY hours, taking vacations, working wherever I want, and whenever I want.

Why would planning events be someone's passion? For people who like to put different things together like a jigsaw puzzle, event-planning comes as a welcome challenge. There are many pieces to a successful event, and for some, it is overwhelming to think of putting them all together—kind of like writing a book.

For an event planner, it is their passion to figure out how to put it together. Event planners have an eye for figuring out how to deliver the type of experience a client is requesting. When a client describes the experience they want to create during and through their event, the event planner immediately knows which pieces to pull together to create that desired experience. The pieces of the puzzle fit together in an intuitive knowing, a gut reaction, to know which pieces to pull together and which ones just don't fit.

After you've read this book, you're going to understand exactly what event planning is, including details like how to find the right venue and how to hire the right team: helpful, like-minded, collaborative vendors. You're going to understand how to assess your financial situation and why it is pivotal to your success to be honest with yourself about it.

You're also going to understand how and when fear and competition get in your way and what to do about it, how to avoid the ten rookie mistakes that an event planner often makes, and you're going to learn how to go from zero to mid-six figures if that's your dream, and how to do it with joy and freedom.

WHAT IS AN EVENT PLANNER AND AN EVENTREPRENEUR?

When people ask me what I do for a living, I am tempted to tell them my job title is Super Woman. This is because when I googled, "What is the definition of an event planner?" this is the result I received: "An event planner structures an event, coordinates all of the moving parts, and makes sure everyone has a good time. Also called convention and meeting planners, they do everything involved in making sure these events go smoothly, including choosing locations, hiring caterers, entertainment, and other vendors." Now, doesn't that sound like a job that requires an army instead of one person?

An eventrepreneur is an entrepreneur who uses his or her passion for events and turns it into a money-making business. As an eventrepreneur, you are applying your event planning skills PLUS business building skills to turn your passion for events into a profitable business.

BECOMING AN EVENT PLANNER AND AN UNSTOPPABLE EVENTREPRENEUR

I have been asked this question many times.

Do you need to take classes and courses? Yes AND no. Personally, I find that what you learn in classes and courses builds a foundation. However, if you don't apply what you learn in a classroom setting, what's the point? You need real-life experience to apply what you learn in a classroom to actual events, and that's how you are going to learn. The best school is the school of hard knocks PLUS the strong foundation you get from books and a good mentor. Good news: you have found both in this book and in me.

Create Your Own Opportunities. Create opportunities to present yourself to the right audience in the right environment. Don't be afraid to ask for help and guidance. When someone gives you an opportunity, you better make sure you don't mess it up because this person will tell the next person what an awesome or terrible job you did, and another opportunity may or may not open up for you.

Learn From Others. Learn from other people who are great in their field of expertise. Ask to shadow them at their events. Don't be afraid to make mistakes and learn from them. Be humble. Being a trainee or an intern is your best opportunity to learn and not be penalized for your mistakes!! Volunteer to plan ANY type of event. You will learn different things from planning different types of events and from working with other planners.

KNOW AND UNDERSTAND YOUR WHY

When I asked the members in our Facebook group why they decided to become event planners, the most common answer was, "Because I love to plan events, and I love seeing my clients happy when they see how beautiful their event turned out."

I even have members who shared that they planned many events for free, just because they enjoyed the entire process of planning an event and seeing how happy their friends and family were while enjoying the event that they planned.

When I asked these same members why they don't monetize their passion for planning events by starting their own event planning business, the common answer is they are afraid they won't make enough money in the business to pay their bills.

Simon Sinek, a world-famous motivational speaker, describes finding your "Why" in a fabulous Ted Talk. He says, "First Why, then trust." In relation to building your eventrepreneur business, Sinek discusses how to find your Why and then how you can differentiate yourself from your competitors when you understand what your Why is.

To start and grow any business successfully, you must align yourself, and I mean ALL OF YOU—your values, your beliefs, and your morals. Sinek brilliantly points out that when it is formed, what an organization does and why it does it are "inextricably linked." As the business grows, sometimes when your stress increases, your passion for this work starts to weaken. It is imperative to the success of your business to remember your Why, and keep alignment with that Why, even when huge challenges arise and the going gets tough. Maintaining belief in your why allows you trust the sometimes-difficult choices/decisions you will be required to make.

Can you imagine having a business where you make enough money to pay your bills, but you absolutely hate working in that business because your mind, your heart, and your soul are not connected to the business? Maybe you have HAD that job already, and you know exactly what I am talking about.

If you make it your goal to help create beautiful events and experiences and understand that this is your ultimate WHY you started the business, you will defy all odds and always do your best to deliver the best experience and the most beautiful event for your client. Trust yourself by trusting your why.

TURN YOUR WHY INTO A PROFITABLE BUSINESS

When people think about opening a business, the first thing they think about is how much money they can make and working their own hours. Revenue is a fundamental piece of building a business and having the freedom to do whatever, whenever you want is a strong motivator. However, many often completely forget WHY they wanted to start a business in the first place, which is the fact that they love planning events and love seeing how happy people are enjoying the fruits of their labor.

So, your Why is wanting to help people plan their events and seeing how happy they are when their events are successful. The joy and fulfillment you get when you see how happy they are is your adrenaline and catalyst for starting your event planning business. The synergy here is to do what you love and get paid to do what you love. The work of planning events is not work, it is your passion, you are now being paid to play! The money will come when you have fun, and you know what really makes you wake up every day to do the same thing day in and day out. Don't lose sight of your Why. If you lose your Why, the rest will be lost, too.

Four Things that Will Happen When You Know Your Why

1. You will be known among your clients and prospective clients as a planner who truly cares about your client's experiences and their events.

2. The universe will reward you with many clients so you can continue to make more people happy. And what comes with more happy clients? Continued work and increased income.

3. You will attract clients who are willing to pay your worth and clients who pay you for your value, not based on price point.

4. With more clients who are willing to pay your worth, the money will roll right into your bank account.

With the money, you can live the life you have always wanted to live.

AHA! Moments

- Learning from actual events will give you more benefit than what you can learn in a classroom.

- Connecting with people will help you learn different materials and create opportunities for you to use.

- Know why you want to be an eventrepreneur. This will help you create the business you want.

CHAPTER 3

BEING A SUCCESSFUL EVENT PLANNER & AN UNSTOPPABLE EVENTREPRENEUR

What makes me a good event planner might not be what makes you a good event planner. We all have our own gifts and talents that can make us stand out in this industry. This is just a simple fact. Our personality, our likes and dislikes, our special skill sets make us all unique. This is what we call our Zone of Genius.

What made me a good event planner is that I am very resourceful and became good at building relationships with clients and vendors.

In my early twenties, my people skills were less than desirable. I am a task-oriented person and often didn't care about the feelings involved, but instead wanted to focus on getting the job done well. Even though I was always concerned about doing a great job, my people skills with the executives in the company I worked for weren't always great because I didn't agree with some of what they were doing or how they were doing it. It is what motivated me to start my own company and do it my own way.

I learned over time that you must build relationships to have a strong support team. When I started M2 Hospitality, I was very clear about the kind of people I wanted to work with on my team, including my clients. Knowing myself and having a strong business plan from the very beginning helped me stay focused on my Why to act in integrity, honoring my strengths as well as my team's and my clients' needs.

Because event planners are such organized people by nature, you think you must have all of your ducks in a row before you market yourself. "I have to have my website all set. I have to be registered as a company. I have to have all of my social media ready. I have to have a ton of experience... When all of that is done, then I can go out and tell people about my work/company." This is untrue. These things are all sensible tasks that can be handled over time. However, the truth is you don't have to have any of them set in stone to begin building your event planning business as an eventrepreneur.

If you don't need any of that, what do you need? You need to know your superpower! For example, what types of events do you like to do? Are you a corporate event planner? Are you a social event planner, like weddings, or children's parties, or adult parties? What kind of style do you like? Do you like a classy, elegant wedding event or do you like the rustic style? What is the thing that you are going to do exceptionally well, which will enable you to enjoy doing what you are doing, while excelling at the same time?

The answers to these questions will affect how you come up with a theme for your client's event, how you find the right venue, how you find the right vendor, how you negotiate, and how you plan for food and beverage. These areas make up just a few of the basic details that are a part of planning for any event. For example, if you put yourself in a situation to plan an event that doesn't suit your skill set or your values, you will find that you are less enthusiastic about the job, and therefore, the outcome will not be as successful.

CONTRACTS

Planning, timing, and energetics all play a role in your success as an event planner, regardless of the type of event planner you choose to be, based on your Why and what you love. Whether you are a corporate event planner or a social event planner, there is one element that underlies every single business transaction you will make: A contract.

One of the most common challenges that event planners encounter is what to include on a client's contract. They have a vague idea of what to include, but anything that requires an understanding of the legal terms, they are completely lost. Thus, event planners can suffer a financial loss if a client disputes event planning services if they are not satisfied. Short of hiring an attorney, you must educate yourself regarding the necessary elements of a legally sound, binding work agreement.

Consider the following elements for inclusion in your contract as you build your business.

Must-Have Items to Include in Your Contract

1. Client Information

Name of the person, contact number, email, and mailing address of the signing party. You need to make sure the signing person is at least eighteen years old and has the authority and capacity to sign on their own behalf or on behalf of the person or company they represent.

2. Your Information

Your name, company name, title, contact number, email, and mailing address. Make sure your title is the same that you put on the registration of your LLC/articles of incorporation.

3. Purpose of the Contract/What the Contract is For

Is this a contract to secure your event planning services, or to secure your decorating services including rental items?

4. Date, Time, and Venue

The start and end times for the event must be listed. The address of the venue must be included, and the name of the event space must be included if the event is happening within a location inside the main event space.

5. **All Products and Services Contracted and Their Prices**

   All products, services, tax, delivery, set up, and tear down charges need to be listed. If you are offering a discount for cash payment, that needs to be listed as well.

6. **Payment Due Dates and Acceptable Forms of Payment**

   Deposit amounts and due dates must be clearly indicated. The method of payment (cash, check, wire transfer) needs to be included. If you are accepting electronic payment, you need to include all the bank details. For check payment, indicate to whom the check must be written.

   If a deposit is not refundable, that needs to be indicated.

7. **Insurance Requirements**

   Some venues will require each vendor and sometimes even the host to provide a certificate of insurance. If the venue you have selected requires that, you need to include that on your contract, and make sure all your clients and vendors are aware of this requirement.

8. **Indemnification Language**

   An indemnification clause will protect you and your staff from any misbehavior or negligence by your client and their guests that resulted in any damage or harm to the property and personnel.

Unfortunately, this sometimes happens, but that is why having this clause in your contract is so important.

9. Termination/Cancellation Language

Can the contract be terminated? If yes, under what circumstances? You need to be very clear about the cancellation policy and the date by which the contract can be cancelled. In addition, you should indicate what is the financial repercussion if the contract is cancelled.

You also need to include a Force Majeure clause. Force Majeure is a common clause in contracts which essentially frees both parties from liability or obligation when an extraordinary event or circumstance beyond the control of the parties, such as a war, strike, riot, crime, epidemic or sudden legal changes prevents one or both parties from fulfilling their obligations under the contract.

10. Intellectual Property

To protect your work, you should have some form of language that clearly states that your work is your intellectual property and cannot be shared or copied.

There are several more items that could be included in the contract, but the ones here are the most common and essential items that must be included. Remember, consulting a lawyer is the best way to receive legal advice and support, but I have been able to incur the extra expense by learning how to read and write contracts on my own, and then have an attorney look over my work instead of having him draft the entire contract on my behalf. Using the suggestions listed here is a great starting point for the contracts for your business, and it will save you some money when consulting with a lawyer as you already have the basic fundamentals covered.

VENUE SELECTION

As an event planner, choosing the perfect venue for your client is a top priority. After all, without a location, there can't be an event. As an event planner, finding the PERFECT venue that fulfills your client's vision AND fits their budget makes you a shining star to your client, and we all want to win the gold star, don't we? So, how do you find the perfect venue for your clients?

There are several factors that you should take into consideration. These are the TOP Five:

1. Location, location, location

Is the venue easily accessible? Do your guests need to do more than one airport transit to get to the destination? Is the venue accessible by public transportation? Is there any parking available onsite? The more accessible your venue is, the more likely it is that guests will RSVP "yes" to attend the event.

2. Existing Facilities and Equipment Included in Venue Fee

Make sure you have a clear picture of the full amenities list of your potential venue for actual physical setting as well as equipment. I had a client who required a multi-media wall for her presentation. I was able to find a venue that had an existing multi-media wall. This venue fee included the use of the wall. By having the event at this venue, we saved the client at least $30,000 for her AV production costs.

3. Any Potential Hidden Fees for the Venue

Sometimes, there are additional fees that are not obvious at the outset of choosing a venue. I had a client who wanted to have an outdoor event at the venue she liked. I was ecstatic to find out the space was available. I immediately asked for a contract to book the venue for my client.

When I saw the contract, I couldn't believe what I saw. The venue charged a fee for the outdoor event space AND for the backup room in case of bad weather. PLUS, they charged an outdoor event set up fee. Not once during the site inspection was I told about these fees.

This experience has taught me to ask venues if there are extra fees that would affect the event's budget.

4. Other Events at the Venue on the Same Day

Are there any other events happening at the venue on the day of your event that may create a conflict?

Once when I was a guest at a wedding, the hotel had two ballrooms separated by a common foyer. As the bride from our wedding crossed the foyer to walk down the aisle, the bride from the other ballroom crossed the foyer to use the bathroom. The two brides saw each other, and the guests of my wedding party gasped.

That precious moment of all eyes on the bride was broken, because now everyone saw TWO brides. I'm sure the wedding planner got an earful from the bride. She should have made sure there was not another bride in the vicinity during the time of the ceremony.

What if you're planning a corporate event? Let's say you're planning a pharmaceutical event for a client. You MUST make sure there are no other pharmaceutical companies in the venue on the same dates as your client's event. That is a HUGE NO-NO.

5. Bringing in Your Own Vendors

Does the venue allow you to bring in your own vendors? I had a client who wanted to do an event at a beautiful venue. She had a personal relationship with a florist and a band and wanted to bring them on for her event. Unfortunately, the venue had a preferred vendor list, and we could only use the vendors on the list.

The venue did eventually allow us to use our own vendor, but my client had to pay them a huge fee to "oversee the load in and load out" process of her vendors.

My client ended up not choosing that venue even though it was perfect for her event.

Venue Site Inspections. As part of your eventrepreneur business, venue site inspections are an important part of an event planner's job. Not only is it important to keep in touch with your client's venue after the venue has been chosen, but it is also essential for your sales and marketing efforts within your own options databases. As an Unstoppable Eventrepreneur, you should be aiming to do at least two to four venue visits a week. These are also known as site inspections in the corporate event planning world.

Why Have a Venue Database? Venue site visits are essential sales and marketing efforts. You need to incorporate them into your sales activity on a regular basis. You should continually be adding new venues to your database. You want to have a wide selection of venues you can propose to your clients. They will appreciate this when they need help sourcing the perfect venue for their event. Venue site visits are also a great way for you to establish a rapport with the venue operators. Having a relationship with the venue will make them more likely to refer business to you.

What Is a Site Visit? A site visit is when you visit a venue to check out the facilities and services that the venue offers. Your main goal is to look at the event space and decide if it will be a good fit for your brand and for your event planning services. Would you offer that location as a venue option for your clients?

What If My Client Has Chosen Their Own Venue? If your client has already secured the venue before hiring you as their planner, arrange for a site inspection. Become familiar with the exact space your client has contracted for their event. This will help you envision the layout of the entire event. You can also plan for any logistic challenges that may arise.

What Should You Include in a Venue Site Visit? The list of things to look for can get rather lengthy, so I will only touch on the TOP three questions that you MUST ASK on a site inspection. I have chosen these questions based on the information that will best serve you and your clients.

1. **Who is on the Venue's Preferred Vendor List?**

   Find out if there are any event planners on the venue's preferred list and if they provide the same services as you. You want to know who the major players are in the industry, so you can start connecting with these planners. Ask if you can have a copy of that list. If you keep seeing the same vendors appearing on the preferred vendor list of several venues, these vendors are worth checking out. They must be doing something right to get on several venue's vendor lists. Start a conversation with these vendors to see if there is a possibility you can use them as one of your vendors. Remember to ask them if they would refer you if someone is asking for an event planner.

2. How Does One Get on the Preferred Vendor List?

Ask how to get on the preferred vendor list so the venue can refer your services to their clients! Also, find out if the venue requires any form of payout/percentage fee if they were to refer a client to you, and they book your services.

I have worked with several venues that have a preferred vendor list, but it is not mandatory for the client to use any of the vendors on that list. I started building a great rapport with the sales and events team at these venues. As a result, they don't send the clients the preferred vendor list; they simply recommend me to these clients. This is the BEST form of leads because you already came highly recommended. This makes it very likely the client will follow the suggestion of the venue operators to work with you.

You MUST continue to show up and nurture that relationship, even after you get on that preferred vendor list! If the venue has a policy that the clients can ONLY use the vendors on the preferred vendor list, this is all the reason you need to show up and build that relationship so you can get on that list!!

3. What are the Venue Restrictions?

This is one of the most important questions that you must include on your site inspection checklist.

If your client has contracted the venue, you need to find out if there are any types of restrictions that will hinder the event logistics. If so, this could potentially incur additional costs for your client. For instance, if the venue doesn't allow vendors to leave any items in the venue overnight, the client will need to pay extra for the vendors to load everything after the event is over, which often means after-office hours for venue staff.

VENDOR SELECTION

Since venues and vendors go hand-in-hand, it makes sense to address them in succession. I get asked all the time, especially from event planners who have just started their event planning business, "Why do I need a vendor list? I have all the inventory that I need to plan an event." I am thinking, *hmmm... your warehouse must be the size of a hanger, and you must be making millions in your business to be able to give me a response like that. Or, you have no clue what you are doing, and you definitely need LOTS of help to grow and run your event planning business.*

An event planner is NOT a one-man show. There is no way that you can do everything by yourself. To be successful financially and to live your dream life running a business that you are passionate about, you need to build an A-Team. The A-Team is you, your staff (if you plan to hire people), and your vendors.

For planners who tell me that they don't need a vendor list, my questions to them will be: Do you have someone on your payroll who knows how to do different types of floral designs, create a backdrop, operate different types of AV equipment, and play different types of music? Do you own different types of furniture, linens, and props that cater to different types of events? Do you have a team of kitchen staff who can prepare different types of foods and beverages?

If your answer is yes, kudos to you! I have a lot to learn from you, because you must be rolling in dough to be able to afford all these overhead costs.

If the answer is no, read on.

Build a Team of Vendors

To be a successful event planner you need to create a team of event vendors you can trust, a team you can count on to help you make difficult deadlines and provide the best in service even in areas you don't directly handle. Be honest, you don't know everything, and you are not good at everything, no matter how smart and talented you are. So, for those mere mortals out there who are not rolling in dough and who have no desire to own or rent a warehouse to store their inventory, let's dive into some of the tips on how to build a vendor list. To build a vendor list, you must first qualify the vendors. Below are some questions you should be asking when you are qualifying a vendor:

1. **Do they align with your brand?**

   What I mean by that is, do they serve the same type of clients as you, provide services at the same venues as you, share the same values as your company, and do they represent their product and services in the same fashion as you?

2. **Do they offer industry rates?**

Do these vendors offer an industry discount for planners, so you have room to mark up the prices for profit?

3. Do they have their staff on payroll or outsource?

If the staff is on payroll, you can be certain that these people understand the value and culture of the company. If they are outsourced, you want to ask if they wear uniforms. You don't want vendors showing up looking sloppy as that is a bad representation of your brand. What's their dress code, and are they trained well for social etiquette, good communication skills, and customer service?

4. How reliable are they?

Are they punctual, and do they clean up after themselves for load-in and load-out? Do they always provide what you have contracted? What is their policy if they overlooked something? How fast can they rectify an unforeseen situation?

5. Do they have a COI (certificate of insurance)?

Some venues require all vendors to have one. Certificates of insurance guarantee that you are covered by liability insurance in the occasion that something happens at one of your hosted events. While you will have your own liability of insurance on file with your venues, you want vendors to have their own certificates of insurance, so they are covered, instead of relying on you to cover them.

6. What's their accounting policy?

Do they offer thirty days credit? How flexible is their payment schedule? How soon do they refund your security deposit?

7. Is there a minimum quantity or dollar amount requirement for each order?

Do they require a minimum amount of the service/product they are providing, or is there a minimum dollar amount requirement to even take your order?

8. How fast do they respond to an inquiry?

This one is HUGE for me. If the response time is slow, that means they are either understaffed, busy, or simply do not care if they get your business or not. Do you want to work with a vendor like that?

9. Do they go above and beyond?

Do they work with you as a part of your team to try and close the deal together? I have vendors who offer 3D floor plans/renderings and do mock set up for my clients, so they can see how the setup and event will actually look. This assists me in helping my clients to understand and visualize the potential result of all of our hard work. A detail like this could help close the sale, benefitting you AND the vendor.

Finding Vendors

Now that we have a strong list of qualifying questions, we must go out there and find the vendors who align with our brand, our desired level of delivery, and potentially, our Why.

Here are a few suggestions: Attend trade shows such as wedding shows and any event industry show where there are plenty of vendors who will have their product and services on exhibit in these shows. This is the best way to see how they represent their brand, product, and services.

Use the Internet! Google vendors near you, stalk them on their social media, look at past jobs, reviews, and testimonials.

Pay attention to referrals by clients, planners, friends and family, venues, and other vendors. Often these people have worked with these vendors and can share their experience with you.

Establishing Vendor Relationships

Here are a few tips for establishing a great relationship with the vendors you think would complement your A-Team:

Make prompt payments. NOBODY likes to work with any-one who pays late. Do you?

Be fair with negotiations. DO NOT squeeze your vendors for a good deal. Respect their work. You don't want people to ask you to discount your work, so why would you want to do that to your vendors?

Be transparent about commissions and referrals. Be honest and tell them that you want a referral fee or commission when you refer a client to them. Or, you will need to mark up their discount prices when you are quoting your clients.

They will understand as everyone is trying to make a living here.

Spread your business. You don't want to depend solely on one vendor. You want to spread the love, so you have good relationships with many vendors. There will always be one favorite vendor that you want to work with, but you don't want to isolate the rest.

Show appreciation. Order vendor meals for them if the setup or if tear-down time is long and tedious. Tip your vendors if they do a really good job. Your clients tip you when you do well, so why wouldn't you tip your vendors?

Schedule a style shoot for collaboration and help promote their brand through your own marketing. This is where you REALLY see who values your partnership. Vendors who want to build a lasting relationship with you and your company will donate their time and inventory/services. The end product will ultimately help everyone to boost their business.

In summary, your vendors should be viewed as an extension of your A-Team and not just someone you contracted for an event. Your clients will see them as part of your team, and you want to treat them like they are your staff. Do you disrespect your staff and treat them poorly? Of course not! When you work with vendors who share your vision of success not just for the events, but also for the company, you have a partnership that goes beyond just business.

PLANNER AND CLIENT RELATIONSHIPS

There are a gazillion event planners out there. How do you differentiate yourself to be the best event planner for your ideal client? Ultimately, a "good" event planner is on the same wavelength as their client but is not afraid to challenge their ideal client with new ideas. At the same time, a good event planner respects her client's vision and budget. You should also be someone who your ideal client likes and respects. Be a person your client will still want to go grab a drink with after the event. Be real, who wants to work with a pain in the tush??

I am a straight shooter and have no filter. I like people who speak English, like laymen, everyday words in English. Don't try to impress me with flowery language, big words, and smoke or mirrors. If my ideal client uses words like "bespoke" or "quintessential," I have already tuned them out.

Do you talk to your friends and family using words like these? Who are you trying to impress? I don't need or want to be impressed or feel the need to impress my ideal client. I want to be able to trust my ideal client and feel comfortable with her and vice versa. Once I feel comfortable knowing that you won't judge me, and I won't judge you, then we can talk. Always remember, it's not always the ideal client picking you, you should also be picking who your ideal client is.

Sad but true story: I had a client for whom I did several events, and all of them were successful. Then, they had a personnel change. This new person loved to be wowed by a big resume, big words, and all the flowery language self-important business people can use to sell themselves.

Because I am who I am, I stopped working with this client because we were no longer compatible. The new events liaison and I were not on the same page. I wasn't too bummed about it, because I knew in the long run, I wouldn't have fun working with this new person. Once you stop having fun, subconsciously your performance will also be affected.

Ask About Your Ideal Client's Exes. No, I am not talking about who your ideal client used to date. I am talking about asking them to share with you the event planners they have worked with (or consulted with) in the past and what they liked or disliked about them. The answers to these questions will give you a good indication of what type of event planner your ideal client is looking for and what they expect you to do for their event.

What Event Planning Experience Is Your Client Looking For? Is having event planning experience important? Yes and no. What exactly constitutes "having experience"? Does "having experience in event planning" mean the event planner must have the experience in planning the type of event your ideal client wants to execute? You may not necessarily have all the experience in the type of event your ideal client is planning. But, if you have the experience in handling certain tasks that your ideal client requires, and your ideal client doesn't mind assigning the rest of the tasks to other team members or doing it herself, that could mean you are an event planner that your ideal client may want to hire. This is especially true when the tasks you can do are in areas in which she is not skilled or doesn't want to handle it by herself or her team.

Can Your Client Trust You? Will you have your client's back and realize her vision? Even if you are not the most experienced, but you know that your ideal client can trust you to do your best, be honest, and communicate clearly and timely, then you will be fine, and the event will be a success.

How Do You Treat Each Other? The success of an event directly connects to how you treat your ideal client and how they treat you. You are a TEAM. You are not just hired help. Your client can't blame you (unless you were negligent and did not do what you were contracted to do) if things don't go well. Your client's job is to make sure you get whatever is needed to make the event a success. Your job is to make your client look good. They give you what you ask for, you go to work with it, your client has a successful event, and everyone wins.

A successful eventrepreneur not only knows their superpower, their ideal clients, and which events they will excel in creating, but has a good sense of time management and planning. There are a lot of things that are going to be vying for your attention as you build your business. You are going to have to decide which things will best support your business and dedicate your time and energy to those things.

Use of energy is something we will discuss a bit later, but bottom line, if something is of importance to you, you WILL make time for it. If you are faced with a task and find yourself saying, "I don't have time," then, you really must be honest with yourself. If that task is necessary to the success of any part of building your business, be it general or client-specific, what you say you really want, deep down, you don't really want that much. Because if you did, you would have made that task a priority, a stepping-stone to manifesting your want.

HOW TO BE MORE PRODUCTIVE

Choosing this book as a resource to build your eventrepreneur business is not a coincidence. One of my assurances to you as your consultant resides in my ability to help you achieve a goal of a six-figure profit, should you choose that. Let me share three tips with you on how you can be more selective, and therefore more productive, so you can find time to work on achieving what you want.

Tip #1: Do LESS, NOT more. Sort out your priorities

When we think about being productive, we always assume we need to do a lot more and add more things to our already over-flowing To-Do List.

The reality is, if you ask very successful people, they DO LESS in their day instead of adding more things to their daily life. What separates them from the rest of the pack is these highly efficient people understand what their priorities are, and they ONLY work on these priorities because they are the BIGGEST DOMINOES that need to be knocked down in order to rapidly move the success needle. They make a "success list," not a "to-do list."

Once these priorities are fulfilled, it creates a domino effect, and the rest of the "other things" become so much easier, and often, no longer necessary.

Start listing all the TOP priorities you need to focus on to reach your six-figure profit. One of these is getting honest about your existing financials, which we will discuss later.

Tip #2: Estimate the time needed to complete each of your priorities.

Once you list your priorities, you need to estimate the time needed to complete each of these tasks. For example, following up with your leads is a priority. Posting content on social media to nurture and engage with your followers (marketing) is a priority. These are just two examples of tasks you should be doing to grow your business to move up to six-figures.

When you believe you have your list of priorities, you need to estimate the time you need to complete each task. Let's assume following up on leads takes thirty minutes and posting on social media takes five minutes (this is assuming content is either already created or is a "spontaneous" organic post). Look at your list of priorities and start giving each one of them an estimated time needed to be completed, and track the actual time taken to complete the task so you can budget your time accordingly moving forward. As you get better at doing a particular task, the time needed to do that task naturally shortens, so now you have more time to do other sales generating activities, or simply, chill!

Tip # 3: Time block for each of your priorities

Now that you know how much time is needed to complete each of the tasks on your priority list, you need to block the times in your day for these tasks, especially tasks that require more than fifteen minutes to complete.

For example, following up with leads takes thirty minutes. You MUST block thirty minutes in your day, every day, preferably the same time each day, to do that task. Mark that down on your calendar, so you do not schedule anything at that time of the day.

If you find yourself having an extra ten minutes between calls/appointments, you know you can use those ten minutes to do a social media post as it only takes five minutes. So, go on LIVE inside your social media and share some nurturing content with your followers during that time.

Takeaways. As an eventrepreneur, you will need to be productive and efficient. These tips are three basic ways to set yourself up for success in planning and time management. There is still the idea that you need to have an overarching, strong business plan for your Why, but these tips help address day-to-day potential time sucks.

One last thing you can do is set a weekly goal on which larger time priorities you want to tackle for that week. At the end of each week, do an audit. Did you complete all the tasks on your priorities list? If not, why?

If you don't take the time to audit your actions at the end of each week, you have no way to measure your productivity and efficiency. How can you expect yourself to be MORE productive and efficient when you don't have a clue why the priorities that you listed are not completed?

Time management and planning are skills that can be taught and learned. They are not easy and require discipline and self-awareness. This is one of the pillars of teaching we focus heavily on inside our Unstoppable Eventrepreneur Mentorship Program™.

WHERE AND HOW YOU SPEND YOUR ENERGY

I previously mentioned rationing your energy as supremely important in building your business. It is supremely important for anything you undertake in your life, and particularly when you are in the process of leveling up in your business/work life. Much like our discussion of time, your energy must be protected and allotted appropriately to your goals and to building a life you love living. In this case, we frame it in terms of being/becoming an eventrepreneur. There are four elements to consider regarding the process of selectively spending your time and energy.

1. **Your Energy**

    When you think about what you want in the manifestation of your business, do you have one foot on the gas pedal and one foot on the brake? For example, you said you want to have your own event planning company; it's the *manifestation* of your dream. What is the thought that follows immediately after you have that manifestation? Is it, "But I don't know how or where to start, and I don't have the money to start the business." Or, "But I don't know how and where to start, and I don't have the money to start the business. However, I am going to figure it out. I will find the resources to make this work!" Do you see the difference between these two thoughts?

The first one, you stop right after you realize you are facing the challenges of not having the know-how and financial means.

The second thought, you acknowledge these challenges, but you immediately think of how you are going to solve the challenges, so you move forward to fulfilling your manifestation.

Too often, people stop at the "but..." They have immediately talked themselves out of their own dreams because they can't see beyond the "but." Creating a successful event planning business requires you to do your solid best at seeing beyond any "buts" that may present themselves.

2. Your Alignment

Is what you are manifesting aligned with your core values, your beliefs, and your actions?

For example, you decide you want to make six figures in your event planning business, but you resist doing the sales activities that's going to give your business positive financial momentum. You are unwilling to acknowledge the simple fact: *Maximum efforts, maximum results. Minimum efforts, minimum results.*

A realistic view of how much you are willing to dedicate to the manifestation of your dream is imperative. If you have a scarcity mindset, or a money-block mindset, when you think about wanting to make that much money, the first thought that comes into your mind is, *"I don't think I could ever make that much money."* This mindset can prevent you from seeing beyond the "but," and doing whatever it takes to bring your dream to fruition. The goal does not align with your current beliefs. Your manifestation MUST align with all of you, and when I say all of you, I mean your mental, emotional, and physical state. These three elements must align to help you achieve your manifestations.

3. Your Actions

Are your actions aligned with the path you need to take to achieve what you are manifesting?

You have decided you want to make six figures for your event planning business. Not only will you need to commit the necessary hours each week but also growing your business to six figures requires consistently doing sales and marketing activities for your business.

Are You Resisting? Say you resist going to networking events, you resist posting on social media, and you resist investing money to attend trade shows. All these are included in the actions you need to take to get you to six figures, but your resistance is hindering you from getting there. If you DO all these things, when you perform these activities, is it to simply check them off your TO-DO list? There is no intention or purpose when you are doing those activities if you do not connect them to your Why. There is no heart and no enthusiasm. You are not fully immersed in the task; therefore, you get distracted and discouraged easily when you don't see immediate results.

Be Intentional. When we are not intentional in our activities, we are just "going through the motions." When you are just going through the motions, the activity itself becomes mundane, and what's worse, when you don't see results doing a mundane activity, you lose motivation.

The fact is the *"mundane"* work you are doing is the foundation you need to build your empire. The "magic" to get to your six-figure event planning company is dressed up as "mundane" work.

Imagine an elite athlete. She practices the same routine, day in, day out, with the same enthusiasm, intention, and focus. Every time she is in practice, she treats it like she is in a competition. She feels the same intensity during practice as when she is competing in the Olympics. Business is just like that. You MUST go in with a mindset that every time you perform the same task for your business, that task is going to catapult you one step at a time to where you want to be. You have to have the same intensity, focus, passion, and intentionality, just like the elite athlete. You get better and more fluid each time, and you start building essential business skills that WILL take you to where you want to be.

4. Your Commitment

Now that you have the energy, the alignment, and the actions all down pat, what about your commitment? When things don't go your way, what do you do? Do you climb back up EACH TIME and keep going, or do you dwell on your "failures," and eventually talk yourself out of your manifestation? Do you start telling yourself that whatever you are manifesting is not that important?

You could just continue doing what you've always done to earn a living. You could continue to earn just what you are earning, without having to strive further for those six figures. You start to negotiate with yourself. You start telling yourself that you *don't really* want the thing that badly, and that you are okay with where you are now. You start to doubt yourself, and if you could really pull this off. You start having all sorts of thoughts: fear of failure, fear of success, you don't really deserve to have what you are manifesting, you are not good enough, insert all the other terrible things we tell ourselves when we are fearful or tired. To have success in your event-repreneurship, with strong business fundamental skills, your Why is part of your plan and helps seal your commitment.

I'm not going to lie and tell you that it is going to be easy to have all these four elements aligned in order to manifest what you envision for yourself. In fact, it is really hard. It takes A LOT of discipline, self-belief, an extremely supportive environment, and a bulletproof mindset to get to where you want to be. The good news is, all these can be created and cultivated.

If you need support in this area, please reach out and find me on Facebook or visit my website to get plugged in to my eventrepreneur community and access all the tools available, including coursework and mentorship.

MARKETING: WEBSITE AND SOCIAL MEDIA

As a business, you have to figure out a way to put yourself out there. Otherwise, you will not attract interest. Making potential clients aware of your presence and your offerings is imperative to any business. Many eventrepreneurs focus on their social media (we will get to this in a bit), but they tend to forget that their company website also needs to be part of their digital platform. To make it welcoming, tell your visitors what services you are offering and who you are trying to attract and provide for.

Things To Consider For Your Website.

There are several things to consider when designing your website. Some of these items include:

- High-quality images that portray your brand and subtly communicate your fees. If the images you have on your site give a perception of luxury, then your website visitors will also have the perception that you are a planner who plans luxury events, which, in turn, means you work with clients with a healthy budget.

- Your font type, font size, color scheme, and the verbiage you use on your website should be congruent across all of your marketing collateral. That's how people will recognize your brand and will immediately associate that brand with you whenever they see different marketing collateral or your website.

- Did you implement Search Engine Optimization for your website? Do you have any keywords plugged at the backend of your website so that people can search for your services and your company pops up on the first page of Google? There are sites that you can visit such as Keywords Everywhere and SEMrush that you can utilize to find the best keywords for your website.

Other Factors to Consider

There are, of course, a lot more factors to consider when creating an effective website that works for your company. The top three factors listed above are the most basic factors to consider. However, I am also going to share three more factors as the core components you have to communicate on your website.

Factor #1 You need to be able to tell them what you do.

That means, what are the services you're providing? What kind of problems do you solve by providing your services, and what would it look like for your target audience if they were to work with you?

Factor #2 Who do you serve? Who is your target audience?

You have to be very specific. If you are a wedding planner and you do rustic style weddings, you want to use language that speaks to potential brides who like the rustic look. You need to know exactly who you're talking to. Being this specific will help people who come to your website know if you are the right person who can help them with their events.

Factor #3 How can they work with you?

Now that your target audience sees what you can do for them, they need to know how to work with you. You need to give specific instructions such as "complete the online questionnaire", "give us a call at xxx-xxx-xxxx" so your audience will know what to do to get in contact with you.

How to Engage Your Website Visitors

What is your call to action for your visitor when they come to your website? Do you have a calendar link where your target audience can schedule a call to speak with you? Do you have a "contact me" box where people put in their info so you can contact them? Do you have an email icon so they can send you an email directly? Do you have a live chat box so they can chat with you instantly?

I particularly love the chat function on the website so your target audience can chat with you in real-time. It's a great feature for the potential client who is hesitant to share their email or is hesitant to get on a call with you. The chat option is just like text messaging or direct messaging. I strongly recommend having the chat option.

To summarize, you need to be able to tell them what you do, who you work with, and how they can work with you. A well-constructed website will generate leads for you 24/7/365.

Social Media

Unless you are living under a rock, most of us utilize one or two social media platforms. If you are an Eventrepreneur, it is absolutely imperative for your business to have a social media presence.

Social media is a free form of advertising for your business, and who doesn't like free stuff? You must have a social media presence for your business if you want to reach out to millions and millions of people across the world as social media has no geographic boundaries.

Social media platforms create multiple opportunities to reach potential clients. These platforms include Facebook, Instagram, Tik Tok, Pinterest, LinkedIn, and YouTube to name a few. To begin, I suggest that if you have not already created a profile for your business on Facebook and Instagram, that you do so right away. It's a great place to start marketing and advertising. Now that you have your social media platform set up for your business, we need to understand how to fully capitalize on the power of social media.

A few factors to consider:

Factor #1: Why Are You Posting on social media?

I like to get feedback from my clients and members of my Facebook mentoring community. When I asked eventrepreneurs why they post on social media, I get answers like, "to gain followers, to get more likes, to grow my social media presence, and to get hired."

All that is fine and dandy, but if you don't have a plan that aligns with your Why and your ideal client, then you could be wasting your time. What's worse is posting stuff that potentially attracts the wrong followers, portrays the wrong impression of your brand, and ultimately, devalues you and your brand.

When you want to post content on your social media, you need to first think of your objective: the end goal of the content on your social media. For example, your end goal is to showcase your knowledge as a party planner, you are asserting your authority in your field. Perhaps you want to create a post with a live video of you describing the Five Basics of a Great Children's Party. You can also use post creation software like Canva to create an attractive graphic if you don't want to do a video. You have options for the delivery of your great ideas. Once you determine what your end goal is, then you progress to the second factor...

Factor #2: What Are You Posting?

When you post something on social media, you need to consider several things. Understand that your social media is not for YOU. It's for your audience. Consider what your followers want to see. What will entertain and engage them? What will cause an a-ha moment for them?

Share content that nurtures them and at the same time builds your authority as the expert in your field. You need to give them content that will show them how you work so that they will see, "Oh, this is how you do it!" It keeps them entertained and engaged, and at the same time, also shows your personality. You can do this at the same time as showing them how you do your work.

If your objective is to show your target audience the work that you do so they are familiar with the type of service you provide, then you should be posting images of the events you have done in the past along with any behind-the-scenes work. This is an easy template: "How do you do x, y, z? Here are some tips for doing x, y, z." Choose your topic: bridal shower, baby shower, wedding. If you are looking to build trust with your audience, you can film yourself at work showing before and after impressions of the space you are working in. Express your gratitude at having the opportunity to do the work that you do in conjunction with the tips you are sharing! This establishes your authority while sharing your personality and providing valuable information.

If your objective is to create engagement, then you should be posting content that encourages your followers to share their input. An easy engagement post template includes asking a question in your post. Ask your followers about the greatest challenges they are currently facing. Tell them that, when you have their answers, you will create some tips or some useful information around what they need, specifically. Extract and compile the information you receive and create your content around that.

If your objective is to build your authority in your field, then share content that nurtures your target audience and content that they find useful.

If your objective is to create sales, then you need to highlight the offer you are selling, the benefits your buyers will experience when they buy your offer and be very clear in the instructions on how they can buy your offer.

Check out my Facebook pages and Instagram for some examples of how I do what I am describing here.

Factor #3: How Are You Engaging with Your Followers?

Whenever my clients in my Events4Anyone: Unstoppable Eventrepreneur Mentorship Program share with me that they are not getting any leads from their social media posts, the questions I ask them include: How frequently do you post? What's the objective of the post? What do you post? Lastly, what do you do with that post after you are done posting it?

Do you track the results of that post? Meaning, did you get any engagements in terms of likes, thumbs up, followers asking questions, or followers making comments? What do you do with those engagements?

Several eventrepreneurs fall into the "post and pray" category. They do a post, then they sit and wait to see how the post "performs." Then, they see several likes, thumbs up, and heart emojis. And then what?

C'mon eventrepreneurs, the ultimate goal of having a social media presence is to get booked for your services, right? Hearts, thumbs up, and emojis are not going to get you booked. You will need to creatively involve yourself with your followers and people taking the time to respond to your posts. You need to engage with your current clients and potential clients.

Open a dialogue with them, send them a DM (direct message), comment on their feed by thanking them for liking your post, and have an Instagram/Facebook DM chat. Ask questions about what they like about your post, and through the DM, you will find out more about your followers, their likes, dislikes, interests, and ways of knowing whether they are one of your ideal clients. All of this information is important data for you as you can use it in the future for doing audience/interest targeting ads for Facebook and Instagram.

These DM dialogues also allow your followers and clients to get to know you better. These conversations provide the opportunity for you to build rapport and trust. They provide you the opportunity to share with them the value you can provide for their events.

In communicating directly with people who have engaged with your posts, you can give them specific instructions on how to get in touch with you. Is there a clear call-to-action on your post for how your followers can reach you to seek out your services? It must be so clearly stated on your post that it's almost dummy-proof, such as, "Contact me at xxx-xxx-xxxx," or "DM me @xyzabc," or "Send me an email at hi@xyzabc.com." You have to make it so clear and so easy that it doesn't require any figuring out on your followers' part regarding how to get in touch with you.

Eventually, you want to get these followers on the phone with you or have them share their contact information with you so you can contact them. The ultimate finale would be to close a contract with them, converting them into paying clients. Otherwise, what's the point of having 1000 likes, when no one books your services?

Other Social Media Considerations

How you decide which social media platform you use to promote your business depends on a few factors. If you are targeting C-level executives, you most likely will find them interacting on LinkedIn or certain professional groups inside Facebook. You most likely won't find them on Tik Tok or Instagram.

On the flip side, if your target audience is millennials, then Tik Tok and Instagram would be your go-to platforms.

If your work is very visual, then Pinterest is the best platform for you.

Once you decide which platform suits your business, you will need to start being "present" on your social media. One of the main challenges that event planners (or any business owners) face is not being "present" on a consistent basis. They will do a lot on their social media one week and then they "disappear" for the next few weeks with zero social media presence.

Consistency Is Key. Developing a strong social media presence requires planning and consistency. You need to commit to a schedule that is realistic for you, so you can commit to that frequency. Posting less each week is better than posting a lot one week and not posting for the next few weeks. Your target audience needs to be constantly reminded that you are still actively in business. When you don't post for an extended period of time, if they are in the market for event planning services, they could stop following you and start following your competitor instead.

What Should You Post? Another challenge that event planners face is not knowing what to post or running out of things to post on their social media. You want to post content that is interesting and beneficial to your target audience.

You should avoid posting what is going on in your personal life on your business social media account unless what you are posting has an entertainment value, or is able to educate or inspire your target audience. For instance, when I am at an event where there is a very innovative set up or the event experience is spectacular, I share that on my social media so my potential client could see the different ways to elevate their own event experience. Put yourself in your target audience's shoes. Do you think they will be interested to know what you had for dinner and where you go for vacation? How is that information helping them to consider hiring you for their event? Most viewers of your social media for business will be asking themselves, even subconsciously, are you able to inspire me, engage with me, and/or educate me?

You want to post content that asserts your authority and shares your expertise. You want to be able to broadcast to a large audience that you are the expert in your field. You want to post content that shows how you work, such as the "behind-the- scenes" footage when you are planning an event.

You want to post content that shows the type of clients you work with, the type of events you do, and share insider's knowledge and tips that will be of value to your target audience. The whole goal of doing all this is to show them you are someone whom they can trust, like, and they can also appreciate the value you bring to them.

One of the biggest mistakes that event planners make is posting images of their work that do not align with their brand or the fees that they want to charge. Whenever you post photos of your work or any form of content that relays your expertise, your target audience subconsciously puts a "price" on how much they will pay for your work.

If the photos do not convey a high-end feel, then you cannot expect your target audience to pay you a high dollar amount for your service. If the content you are sharing is not of value to them, then they will not trust you to plan their high-end event.

Analyze Your Social Feed

As event planners, we sometimes have "blinders" on. We think that our work is beautiful, and we deserve to be paid the fees that we want to charge. Often, the opposite is true in that you are not the best person to evaluate your own work. Sometimes we think a post conveys a certain message, when in fact, we miss our target. Ask a friend or acquaintance to take a look at what you have posted on your social media and ask them to give you some feedback. Ask them to share how much they would pay for your work based on the photos of your past work and the content you are sharing on your social media. You may be surprised by what they share. Having an observer evaluate how your events come across through their perception of them on social media is a great tool.

Some social media outlets also provide analytics on how well your social media is performing. On Instagram, you will be able to tell where most of your followers are from, their gender, age group, and the times they are active on that platform. This information is extremely valuable as you can implement a sales strategy based on the data. For instance, I can see that many of my followers' engagement with my posts are between the time frame of 9:00 a.m. -10:30 a.m., so I will schedule my post to be published between that time frame so I can appear on the newsfeed of my audience. Social media is a great way to promote your business, but you need to have a good understanding of who your target audience is, which platform to use, when to post, how often to post, and lastly, what to post. Once you have all these factors dialed in, you may just have found yourself a money-making machine.

FACEBOOK ADS

Many eventrepreneurs use Facebook and Instagram ads to get leads for their business. Unfortunately, many of the event planners I speak to tell me that it didn't work for them. They say nobody clicks on their ad, or people click on their ad, and then these people ghost them.

Sidenote: If you don't already know, Facebook owns Instagram. When you run a Facebook ad, it will automatically run on Instagram too unless you manually disable the function. There is a certain finesse required to use Facebook Ads to their greatest potential in creating a pipeline for your business and for converting followers into clients. It is important to know how to use this tool appropriately and efficiently.

Potential Facebook Ad Mistakes

When I ask event planners to tell me exactly what was included in their ad and what was their call to action, I get a blank stare. These eventrepreneurs have no idea what I'm talking about. They have no idea how to use Facebook ads to get more qualified leads.

Often inexperienced marketers think creating a Facebook ad means simply advertising the services they offer.

When people click on the ad, they go to the company website. These same eventrepreneurs assume that when someone gets to their website that they will automatically complete the contact form to request a consultation.

Oh noooooo...that is THE most common mistake that the majority of eventrepreneurs make when they run an ad to try to obtain leads. They hope and pray that someone will contact them for a consultation. These Facebook ads newbies have no idea what makes someone click on an ad or what to do once someone does click on their ad. They also have no idea who is seeing their ad.

Running Facebook Ads

Before investing in ads, answer the following questions for yourself in alignment with your overall plan.

1. What challenges are your potential clients facing or trying to solve?

2. What solutions are you providing that can help your potential client solve their challenges?

3. What would the life of your potential client look like if they were to work with you to solve their challenges?

You MUST highlight these three factors. This is the first step to create a winning ad. If you only talk about the services you offer, you have no idea if the people who are seeing your ad need your services.

This is why no one is clicking on your ad, or you get people who are not your ideal client clicking on your ad, then ghosting you. If you are intentional about who you are trying to attract and you highlight the possible challenges that your target audience is facing when planning their event, you are directly "talking" to your ideal client. Then, you will get the attention of your ideal client.

If you are a corporate planner, you want to target corporations. If you are a wedding planner, you target and attract couples. If you are a children's party planner, around

April and May, you can target graduation parties to access busy parents. When you follow-up with the engagement on your posts, you can begin conversations around whether or not your potential client knows how many people they want to invite, what kind of food they want to serve, whether they want to host in a restaurant or their home, whether they have a budget, and if they know how these different choices will affect their budget.

First, identify who your target audience is. When you know your audience, you can direct Facebook to show your ads to these groups of people. You can also plan what makes sense to happen after someone clicks on your ad.

Put yourself in the shoes of the person who clicked on your ad. They want more information about what you are showing in your ad. For example, let's say your ad talks about helping them make a budget for their wedding. When they click on your ad, they are expecting to see something that explains how to make a wedding budget. If you send them to your website, are they going to a page that shares info about how to make a wedding budget? Don't send people to your company website and let them wander around, hoping that they will complete your "Contact Us" form for a consultation. Instead, have a very clear call to action on the ad that says something like, "Click here to get the free checklist on how to make a wedding budget."

Once they click on the link, you can direct them to your website, BUT there should be a pop-up window that will prompt them to put in their name, contact number, and email address to receive the free checklist. By doing this, you are building your email list. You will have a way to connect with these Facebook ad leads. After they submit their information, they get to check out your website and see the work you do, testimonials, and galleries of previous events for different clients. Thus begins the nurturing process of building the like, know, and trust elements of your relationship with your leads.

AHA! Moments

- Suffering a financial loss is not worth the headache. Make sure you understand the necessary elements for a legally binding contract.

- Developing relationships with venues and vendors will help you attract the types of clients you want and help you build your team.

- There are four elements—energy, alignment, action and commitment—contributing to the success of your business. Examine each to determine if your energy is working against you, how to better align it, what actions to take on your path, and how to stay committed to your passion.

- It is important to consider your website as part of your digital marketing. Take advantage of free promotion through social media and make sure that if you pay for a Facebook ad, you thoroughly answer the questions of what your customer needs and how you meet that need with your service.

CHAPTER 4

WHAT KIND OF EVENT PLANNER ARE YOU?

Figuring out what kind of event planner you want to be requires patience with yourself, and your clients, as you build your eventrepreneur six-figure business. You might work with clients that you love, and you might work with clients that you hate as you figure out this piece of your business.

In the beginning, you might be prone to taking any event or client simply at the prospect of making money, or simply for the experience. This is okay, but the sooner you can dial in what types of events will be your specialty, the sooner you can dial in your business to your plan, in alignment with your overall financial, organization, and life goals.

On what kind of event planning should I build the foundation of my business? This is one question that I get asked all the time. The answer is finding out the WHAT, WHO, WHERE & WHY.

WHAT EVENTS WILL YOU PLAN?

The first question you need to ask yourself is what events do you like to plan? You must be very specific. If your answer is all types of events, then you are not being honest with yourself. Do you like planning ALL types of corporate events, including several day conferences, product launches, galas, sales retreats, and day meetings? Do you like planning ALL types of weddings, including Indian weddings, Chinese weddings, American weddings, glitz and glamour weddings, big weddings, small weddings, rustic weddings, and boho weddings?

You have to really think about this. If you end up doing everything, you will be known for nothing. Ask yourself, what type of event style are you drawn to? If you like to plan weddings, what is your favorite type of wedding that you like to plan? Rustic weddings? Big weddings? Backyard Weddings? Glitz and Glamour Weddings?

You can't be good at everything and be all over the place. Yes, you may be able to do it all, but if it's not your favorite type of style or events you like to do, you will get burnt out very fast and will start to resent what you initially said you love to do.

Once you determine the type of event you like to plan and the event style, then you can begin to examine WHO will be your client.

WHO IS YOUR IDEAL CLIENT?

Very often, your ideal client is some version of yourself. Your best client is someone who shares the same vision as you and most likely shares the same values and some personality traits, as well.

So, if you like the rustic look and like to plan events that support that theme, your ideal client should also like events that support that casual, laid-back theme.

Once you attract ideal clients who share the same vision as you and like the same things as you, it will be so much easier for you to convert them into actual paying clients.

On the flip side, if you are into planning weddings with the rustic look, and you receive an inquiry from a potential client who wants you to plan a corporate gala event in a glitzy hotel, you will need to consider this lead carefully. She wants a look that incorporates a lot of high-tech animation and imagery, and the decorations to be all glitz with lots of bling. Do you think you will enjoy planning that event?

Ultimately, the type of events you want to plan need to align with your passion. Because if you are planning events that align with what your passion is, then it's not work.

Where Will You Find Your Ideal Clients?

Put yourself in the shoes of the person who wants to use your services.

If you like rustic-looking events, that means you like nature, you like earth-tone colors, you like things that have a natural texture, and you most likely enjoy being outdoors.

So, look for event venues that offer this type of ambiance and offer your services to these venues. The brides who want to have their weddings with that type of look will be looking for venues that offer that type of atmosphere. You won't find your brides who like the rustic look booking a venue that is ultra-modern looking with lots of glass and bright lights. These venues with outdoor space or have natural landscaping are venues that you want to establish a great relationship with so they can refer you to your ideal clients.

Why You?

Interview yourself. Why would YOU buy from you? What is unique about you? You have to be very specific. Answers like, "Oh, I provide the best customer service, and I will provide a memorable experience for your event," won't cut it. The gazillion planners out there all say the same thing.

What makes you different from other planners? What sets you apart and above other planners? What types of challenges are you trying to solve for your ideal client? By solving those challenges for your ideal client, how would that make your ideal client feel?

Interview your best client. In their testimonial, find out why they picked YOU to work with and not other planners. What problems did you solve for them? How did they feel when you solved their challenges? What specific information from your satisfied clients will help you create language that will appeal to similar clients in the future? Use the exact verbiage that your best client used and post it all over your marketing collateral and social media because your client just highlighted your "superpowers." You want to broadcast your superpowers EVERYWHERE.

EVENT PLANNER VS EVENT DESIGNER

I put a poll in our Facebook group asking our members if they are an event planner, an event designer, or both. OR, if they had a clue that there is a difference between the two? My suspicions were proven right. Several members could not differentiate between the two. Something so obvious, yet so confusing.

Event planners create the organization and structure for how the event will need to run. They pull all the moving parts together so that the event can proceed through its time frame most successfully. Event designers help make sure that the atmosphere and mood surrounding the moving parts create a beautiful, intentional aesthetic that matches the client's desired outcome. If an event planner ensures the successful proceeding of the event, then the designer ensures that it happens in keeping with the client's perceived vision.

Does Event Planning Mean I'm an Event Designer?

Many planners think of themselves as event designers, especially when they first start their event planning company. You feel the need to be everything and do everything yourself.

I get asked this question a lot: "Don't I need a decoration inventory to start my event planning company?" Another popular concern: "I don't have the start-up capital to start my event planning company."

Hello, it's called an event PLANNING company, not an event decorations company... get it? As an event planner, your job is to plan, organize, strategize, see, and communicate the vision. You share your vision with an event designer who is the creative brain in the event planning process, and the event designer works with different vendors to turn that vision into a reality.

When you first start out in your business, especially if you plan small social celebrations or events like birthday parties, you feel that it's part of your event planning responsibility to be physically designing and putting up the decorations.

If you want your business to stay small, play small, and your business is a hobby more than a business, then yes, you are a planner and a designer. However, if you want to turn your event planning company into a thriving business, then stick to planning. Your client pays you the big bucks to plan, strategize, organize, and find the best vendors to execute your and their vision. This means you can find a designer you trust with your vision as one of your vendors. Now, I am not saying that you can't make the big bucks as an event designer, what I am saying is pick your path, which is where your PASSION actually lies, planning or designing? If you are an event planner AND have the creativity to create event designs, but you know you prefer to stick to planning, what you can do is to find vendors who share the same vision as you for your event designs and use those vendors to physically carry out your event design.

GROWING YOUR EVENT PLANNING BUSINESS

Your client is not expecting you to be the one designing the event. When I say designing, I am talking about the decoration elements that could elevate the experience of the guests such as color and event theme, types of specialty furniture, linens to use, floral choices, draping, and lighting.

As the planner, you have a general idea of how the event should look based on your client's vision. Your plate is already full of all the planning, strategizing, organizing, coordinating, and communicating, so please leave the design specifics to someone who is an expert in that field, such as an event designer.

Do not underestimate the importance of understanding this difference. When we attempt to take on too much, as with any area of our life without a cultivated awareness, we can spread ourselves too thin and take ourselves out of our own Zone of Genius before we even realize it has happened. If we do this too often, our events might not go as smoothly as we need them to in order to cultivate the clients we want to attract to grow our business to six-figures. Honestly, a more refined, smoothly executed event goes a long way toward this end. This will not happen if you are pulled in too many different directions at one time.

Hiring An Event Designer

If your client has the budget to hire an event designer, DO IT! Your client can share her vision for the event, your job as the event planner is to put together the best "team," a.k.a. your vendors which include your event designer and the vendors you and he/she use to elevate your client's vision.

If your client doesn't have the budget to hire an event designer, your job as the event planner is to communicate your client's vision to your trusted vendors, which include the vendors you use for all your decor elements like your florist, your specialty furniture and event decor props rental vendors, and your audio-visual vendor, to name a few.

An event planner is like the General. The General will pass the commands down to the Lieutenants. One of the Lieutenants is the event designer. The event designer follows whatever the event planner asks him or her to do. If you are missing a lieutenant, then you need to communicate your client's vision very clearly to your "captains," which are your individual vendors.

As an eventrepreneur and successful business owner, the ability to delegate responsibilities to the appropriate person, like an event designer, becomes extremely important when you are looking at moving your business into a six-figure category. Up leveling requires you to be very savvy in knowing yourself, knowing your abilities, knowing your skill set, and knowing where your energy and capital will be best appropriated. This involves being very honest with yourself about your current financial standing as well as being honest about what support you will need to take your business to a higher level. This is the subject of the next chapter.

AHA! Moments

- Determining the type of event you like to plan and the event style will help you examine WHAT type of event planner you are and WHO will be your best client.

- Your best client is likely to be someone who shares the same vision as you, shares the same values, and some personality traits, as well.

- Whether you are an event planner, an event designer, or both, you can't be everywhere doing everything all of the time. Attempting such a feat draws your energy too thin and it will show in your events. Hire and work with vendors that understand the client's vision.

CHAPTER 5

UNDERSTAND YOUR FINANCIALS AND RISK APPETITE

"You have to have money to make money..."

"Good as gold..."

"Champagne tastes on a beer budget..."

There are as many cliches about money as there are actual truths and principles about the way finances function in our lives. Regardless of your past experiences with money, regardless of how you were raised to look at and approach money, regardless of any of your past negative OR positive conditioning around dealing with money, the fact remains that you have to have a clear view of your financial health and function, or dysfunction, to build a strong, healthy, sustainable future for your eventrepreneur business.

KNOW YOUR FINANCE AND RISK APPETITE

Basic requirements for business finance: You must know how much you are bringing in each month and what are your expenses, so you know your net. This is your profit. It is the bottom line, financially. There are different allocations of funds that happen when you own a business, and there are ideal percentages that will be allocated for different things. However, there is also a mindset that goes along with being able to manage the money coming into your business.

I am going to give you a basic example. You have $1,000, your fee for an event, coming into your business. Of that $1,000, fifty percent goes to you. The other fifty percent should be used for your business: Thirty percent for labor, ten percent for technology, and ten percent to marketing, advertising, or entertaining your clients. Everything has its own category, and you will know where each piece of the other fifty percent goes.

Often what happens when we are first starting our business, we take one hundred percent of the fee into our personal bank account and spend it from there on whatever we want. I understand this. However, for building your business to a six-figure salary, there are other things that need to be managed and considered. I include the percentages for labor, technology, and marketing because those are the main expenses you will have for building and growing a sustainable event planning company. I have information available on how to calculate all of this… fixed costs, variable costs, and how it should all look for healthy business finance. Beneath all of this, there must be a mindset for strategic planning.

A strategic planning mindset for finance might not come naturally to you; it's okay. You will learn. First, let's look at some of the common ways we undermine our financial growth without realizing it.

Mindset #1

You want to do everything yourself, even if it is not your Zone of Genius. For example, you want to create and maintain your own website, or a social media content calendar. A lot of new event planners have a challenge with these two pivotal business items, but then, you resist spending money to pay someone else to help you with them. So, you think, "I will do it myself to avoid the expenditure."

When the time comes to perform the necessary activity for these tasks, you find yourself frustrated to the point of upset and cursing at the computer! Then what happens? You waste even more time in resisting completing the task because these tasks are difficult for you. This causes you to transfer your frustration, and you begin to assume that ALL parts of business building are difficult. Then, you stop doing any of it. Once resistance starts, resentment builds.

How do you stop this? Start looking at how you are spending your money and find the cash flow to pay someone to help you. Look at your credit card, see where you can cut spending to allot the money back into your business to pay for the support you need.

Mindset #2

If you are building an event planning business as a side hustle, you hate your "day job," because it is robbing time away from allowing you to build your business.

How do you shift this outlook? Realize that you have your job to help you finance your passion. You are working in the job so you can have the money to hire the help you need, when you are managing it well. You can have the money to hire a website builder, a social media person, or to pay for a trade show! Appreciate that this job exists as part of your path to owning your own business.

Now, there is another way to approach business building, which involves quitting your job instead of growing event planning as a side hustle. I am not advocating that you do this, but I am going to inform you that it depends on your risk appetite and your ability to handle the risk that this approach involves. I would only suggest you take this approach if you have enough in reserve financially to pay all your bills for six to nine months, and you can handle the kind of pressure that comes from knowing you will need to go out, hustle, and make it happen pretty quickly. This approach is not for everyone.

If your risk appetite is not large, know that your "day job" is helping support you in your eventrepreneurship until you are ready to become a full-time CEO.

Mindset #3

"No one can do it better than me."

Does this sound familiar? You hesitate hiring someone to help you run your events because no one can do it as well as you can, or if you step away and let someone else do it, something will go wrong. Or you can't hire someone else to do your website because no one could possibly understand your vision.

When you have this mindset, your business is your job, and you have given yourself a set of golden handcuffs. If you want your business to grow and to live the life you want to live, you have to find people you trust to support what you need in your business. There are good people available to do the kind of work you need done! Web designers, social media managers, event designers, bloggers… they are all out there, doing their work in their own Zone of Genius, prepared to do what is NOT in yours. Let them.

This mindset causes counterproductivity. Instead of having the freedom to live or to travel the way you wanted to when you created your business in the first place, you are now tied to the business, the way you felt when you were working for someone else.

Begin to think about the things you as the CEO must do, and what are the things you could train someone else to do. At M2 Hospitality, my events business, during peak season, I am running four to seven events a day. How on earth could I have this mindset and have all of these be successful events? There are not seven of me.

I have created a team of operations people that I trust to help create the best work my business can create. I train them to watch me work. They understand my detailed notes. I show them how I create and how I do things during events, and then, I let them work events on their own, in charge.

I make sure my clients know that my operations team is in charge, from the beginning, so that they understand I have someone working with me to help create their successful events. I even make phone calls with my operations person on the call with me and my client in the planning stages. The operations person can then create the event proposal; they submit the proposal to me for approval, and then they send it to the client for the sale. Look for people who are good at doing the things you are not great at. Look for people who can see things that maybe you do not see. They will complement you in your position beautifully.

These employees are contractors who have filled out a W-9 with all of their mailing information and social security number or tax ID number. At the end of the year, you send them a form 1099 for them to complete their taxes. If they earn less than $600 from you, you don't have to send them the 1099. If it is more than $600, you should send them a 1099. You will report the expense, no matter how much money you pay them.

Contractor rules are pretty simple, but in the state of California, it can get tricky. You should always ask an accountant if you have a situation about which you are unsure or need more advice.

Where do I get the money to pay my operations person? I incorporate their fee into the planning fee I charge my client. If it is an internal work that is not client related, like website building or social media manager, remember the thirty percent allocate of your fee that you put into your business account to help pay for your labor? There you have it. It may not be financially possible for the first few events but knowing that you will be able to do this as you begin to earn and wisely manage your money will help you grow to the six-figure level you are looking to reach.

Mindset #4

You over-zealously invest in something or in the business.

I would always encourage you to invest in yourself and in your business, but before you spend large amounts of money in the hopes of eventually making money, or earning back that investment, I think you should ask yourself some questions: Why are you investing in this thing? Software, a mentorship program, a course? How will you implement what you have invested in? How would you evaluate whether the investment is worth it? Do you have a benchmark for yourself where you can evaluate whether the investment is working for you? The results of your investment could be financial, and the results could be transformational. Sometimes the results include both.

When I pay someone to do a job for me, I know what my return on my investment is (ROI)... being able to pay someone $150 to do a job for me has given me the time to go and earn $1500 on behalf of the company. This is my ROI. When you are investing your money in yourself or for your business, you have to be able to think forward and assess what will be your ROI.

Moving away from any of these mindsets requires courage to look at yourself honestly and become aware of when you might be engaging in any one of them. Making the shift to managing your financials for a six-figure business growth means letting go of the illusion of needing to be in control of every single element of your business, or tripping over $1000 to save $100. It gets easier the more you have to do it, and by growing your confidence, trusting yourself, and trusting your people, your leaps of faith will pay off.

Risk Appetite. One way to mitigate your financial risk in creating your event planning business involves establishing a partnership. Especially, if you are planning to quit your job, one way to mitigate that risk is to find a business partner that can invest in the business or share the cost of the business. Having a business partner is not for everyone, but there are a few ways to evaluate whether this path is for you or not. As a business coach for event planners, this is a scenario discussed often in my online community. My advice on this is clear.

DO YOU NEED A BUSINESS PARTNER?

Instead of asking if you need a business partner for your event planning company, you should be asking WHY you think you need a business partner.

Let me guess, are you thinking that you will need a huge financial commitment to start your business? Don't believe it when people tell you that you need an office, inventory, or a venue before you can start your own event planning company.

I started my event planning business many years ago with just my phone, my laptop, and A LOT of time spent networking and building relationships with venues, vendors, and potential clients. There is no need to have a partner to share the financial burden just because you have this belief that it cost a bomb to start an event planning company.

Fear of Failure. Are you afraid that you can't pull off building an event planning company by yourself, so if you fail, there is someone next to you? Is that business partner your security blanket? The good news is, if you pick the right partner, you will NOT fail. If you pick the wrong partner, you will feel doubly horrible because how could two brains not figure out how to start and build an event planning business?

The Only Reason To Have A Business Partner

I am going to kill the suspense and make it simple here for you my fellow eventrepreneurs. The ONLY reason you should have a business partner is when the business partner fills a void in the part of the business that you cannot fill, for whatever reason. For instance, if you are absolutely disastrous in organizing your work, have zero interest in handling ALL the day-to-day logistics of running the business, such as the accounting work, setting up procedures and protocols, or managing staff, you might consider a partner whose skill set matches the completion of these tasks. If you ONLY want to do sales and marketing and be involved in the event planning process, then you may want to look for an individual who can take over the rest of the administrative work needed to run an event planning business.

Having said this, there is no need to have a business partner. You could easily hire a virtual assistant on a full-time or part-time basis in order to handle the pieces of paperwork and record keeping that you don't want to do.

Relationship With A Business Partner

Having a business partner entails a lot more than just having another person to bounce ideas off and share responsibilities with. It involves legalities that need to be ironed out before the company is incorporated. It requires you to draft an operating agreement that will detail percentages of ownership each of you will have.

If you are incorporated as an LLC or a partnership, you do not need to be equal partners. Several companies on and off the record will use the percentage division to guide them on splitting profit, expense, and responsibilities. The operating agreement will also need to list who is responsible for doing what.

I have seen many business partners buyout their business partner for sole ownership. I have seen voluntary exits of one partner because of disagreements once the business got going. Someone is not doing what they are supposed to do according to the original agreement, or someone is unwilling to uphold certain financial commitments. It can get really messy.

You and your potential business partner must have values that align. Both of you must agree how you want to grow the company, be very clear about the financial commitment when you first start the company, AND once the business is in motion, the responsibilities assigned to each of you and commitment to carrying out the responsibilities as listed on the operating agreement. It is always best to put together a business plan where both of you can lay out EVERYTHING needed to start and grow the business in alignment with one another as both of you have a vested interest in how things evolve.

Lastly, before you decide to have a business partner, ask yourself three questions:

1. Why do I need a business partner?
2. What will the business partner do?
3. How would his/her presence help me in the business?

Ultimately, if the main reason you think you want to have a business partner is to have physical and emotional support, there is NO need to have a business partner. There are other ways to have these needs met, to include joining the online eventrepreneur community. Access to this information can be found at the end of the book.

HAVING A VENDOR PARTNERSHIP

Having a clear financial picture of your business and what it can and cannot afford supports your ability to negotiate for what you want and need as a part of doing business. This includes being able to find the best deal for the services your business requires as well as the services sought on behalf of your clients.

Vendor Partnership Revisited. Before I decide to negotiate contract terms with any vendors, one of the factors that I consider is whether or not I see myself entering into a long-term business relationship with them. To determine if we can establish a long-term partnership, I consider if the vendor is aligned with my brand and my core values for my event planning business. I would only negotiate for vendor terms with vendors on my preferred vendor list because these vendors are the ones I have carefully handpicked to form a lasting win-win partnership.

Vendor Negotiations. Once I determine a vendor is one I want to work with long-term, I will negotiate for three main items that make a huge impact on my event planning business. These are industry rate, payment terms, and collaborations.

Industry Rate

If I know that I will be using this vendor on a frequent basis, I will ask for a vendor discount or industry rate. This means the vendor will be giving a discount on the retail rate that she charges her end consumer.

Many vendors do not offer industry rates when you are new in the business as they can't take your word that you will refer them enough business to make up for the discount by giving you an industry rate.

One way to work around this involves asking for a discount when the dollar amount for an order surpasses a mutually agreed upon dollar amount. After a few business transactions, you will build the trust and transaction history for them to reference, and then you will be in a better position to ask for an industry rate that will be applied for each of your orders, regardless of your order total. To maintain this vendor term, you should try to uphold a certain amount of business given to this vendor, just to be fair to them. Also understand, that if the event falls on a peak date, don't expect the industry rate to be applied as it's fair game for everyone in this case.

Payment Terms

For payment terms for a preferred vendor, I ask for thirty days' credit instead of having to pay the entire order before the event. Again, if you are new in business, these vendors do not know you, so they often won't be willing to extend the thirty days grace. This is something that you can build over time.

A potential work-around for this situation is to ask for fifty percent down, and fifty percent due immediately after the event. Then, you move on to ten to twenty percent down, and the rest due after the event. Once you build up enough credit history, you can then ask for the thirty days credit.

Know that this is probably one of the most difficult terms to negotiate, because everyone wants a positive cash flow for their business. You have to be extremely conscientious in making sure that you ALWAYS pay on time to keep a good credit standing with ALL your vendors. You screw up with one vendor, word can spread, and you can bet that no vendor will ever extend this thirty-day grace period for you again.

Collaborations

Lastly, collaborations with preferred vendors benefit both businesses. Collaborating with one of your preferred vendors can be fun at the same time as growing and supporting both of you. I will ask my vendors if they do collaborations with me when I need their services/items for style shoots, when I host a booth at a trade show, or when I need them to sponsor their services/items when my preferred venue partners host a client appreciation event. Any of these scenarios provide great opportunities to collaborate with a vendor that I love. In return, I will include their company name on any of the marketing materials for the sponsored event as well as my social media marketing posts for the event.

Always remember, you must first be a GREAT vendor to work with, before asking anything from your vendors.

PRICING EVENT PLANNING PACKAGES

It can be challenging to figure out how to price your event planning packages because there isn't one "standard market rate" that eventrepreneurs can reference. This pivotal piece of your business is a combination of the effort and skill required for the event combined with the size and length of the event plus any special requests from your client, mixed in with making sure that you are charging what you are worth. Often and sadly, eventrepreneurs go into a price bidding war to win a job, which should never be the way to grow your event planning business.

Potential Pricing Mistake. One of the most common mistakes that I see many new eventrepreneurs make when pricing their packages rests on the idea that they checked out the website of their competitor. They do some snooping around, find out their competitor's offerings and their price points, and then they offer the same event planning services as their competitor BUT at a lower price! The reason these eventrepreneurs feel like they should not or could not charge the same price point, or more than their competitor is because they feel that they are new in the business, so they should "discount" their prices so they can win the business. That is total BS if you ask me. If you have the skill set and experience to perform the services listed in your package, then there is no reason to price yourself lower than your competitor or below the market rate for the services being offered.

Hiring Your Event Services

Your potential client is not going to make their decision based on how long you have been in business. The decision to hire you (or not) is based on how much they believe you can help them in delivering a flawlessly memorable event and if your personality jives with theirs.

Your ideal client doesn't care about how long you have been in business or how many certifications you have. You can be in business for decades of time and have several designations after your name such as CMP, CWEP, or CEP, but if your potential client does not feel that they can trust you or think you can provide the value they are looking for, and more importantly, they don't think your personality blends well with theirs, then you won't get the business.

How To Price Your Packages

There are several ways to price your packages, but I am going to share with you a simple, two-step process to help you correctly price your packages.

Step #1: Analyze your skills and experience. Then determine what type of event planning services you like and want to provide.

You should, first, evaluate your event planning skill set and experience. Once you analyze and acknowledge what type of event planning skills and experience you have, decide on the services you can and would like to provide and know you can deliver those services confidently.

Please do not feel like you have to offer the same, if not more, event planning services compared to your competitors in order to win the business. If you are not skilled at certain services that your competitors are offering, or if you do not have the bandwidth to provide those services, then you should not include those services in your package.

Know that if you decide to include services that you are ill-equipped to provide or do not have experience delivering, you will not be able to deliver the service smoothly. If it goes badly, you can lose the trust of your client almost immediately, and that will have a negative impact on your reputation.

You need to be very honest with yourself. Have an understanding of what type of event planning services you enjoy providing, and then gauge your skill level and bandwidth. If you can provide what you say you want to provide in your packages, great! However, you do not want to follow the trend, copy the competitor, and create "false advertising" for services that you resist to deliver or can't deliver just so you can keep up with the Joneses.

Step #2: Estimate how many hours you need to deliver your event planning services.

Once you determine the type of event planning services you want to provide in your package, create a time estimate of how long it is going to take for you to carry out each of those services.

To be a successful eventrepreneur, you have to know how long it takes for you to complete each event planning service. For example, you should have an idea of how long it takes for you to do venue sourcing, vendor negotiations, drafting a planning timeline, as well as an event timeline, and making an event budget.

Look at the services you list in your package, then allocate the number of hours needed to complete each service. Then, calculate the total number of hours needed to complete all the services listed in your package. Add a twenty percent buffer to that. So, if you calculated forty hours needed to complete all the services listed in your package, add twenty percent to that so you will budget forty-eight hours to provide all the services listed on your package. If you are charging $75 an hour, then you will need to charge at least $3,600 for your package to compensate for your time. If you are including supplies and decoration items in your package, you need to add the cost of those items into your package fees, as well. If the supplies and decoration items cost $500, then your package fee will be $4,100.

A lot of eventrepreneurs make the mistake of taking a potential client's budget, estimating the cost of supplies, and then the balance becomes their profit a.k.a., their fees. They are doing the calculation backward. This is a HUGE NO-NO. This is one of the main reasons why many event planners feel that they work their tooshie off, and they make little to no money!

Raising Your Fees Without Guilt

When you raise your fee, three wonderful things will happen:

1. You start attracting your ideal client.

Clients who are used to paying top dollar for a service and understand they are paying for the value and the experience they can receive by hiring you. Their mentality is very different from clients who have a low budget who will nickel and dime you.

You will notice that clients who are willing to pay a higher event planning fee or have a higher budget for their event approach the entire planning process differently. They act more professionally, for example, they are almost seldom late for appointments, they will follow your directions, and they will usually not second guess you. They will also have as little involvement in the planning process as possible because they know they have hired an expert to plan their event. As such, there is not much they have to worry about or be involved in... they are not as inclined to micro-manage your work. These clients pay you top dollar to take away the stress of planning the event themselves. They trust your judgment, respect your work, and will adhere to the timelines you share with them. They know they have to give you all the information in a timely fashion in order for you to plan a flawless event, otherwise, their money will go to waste.

You feel more valued for the work you produce, and you start feeling more confident about yourself and your business.

When a client pays you a high event planning fee, you subconsciously will feel like you have to "step up your game." You start taking YOURSELF more seriously. You start thinking like a CEO, you make decisions like a CEO, and you act like a CEO. You walk around with an air of confidence, and people will start noticing you. Your mindset also starts to change. You no longer think small, play small, and act small. You understand and acknowledge your worth. You no longer think that you need to go after EVERY client. You learn how to say NO to the wrong client, so you can reserve your time and resources to say YES to the right client.

2. You WORK LESS and EARN MORE

If your income goal is $100,000, and you are charging $1,000 for each client, you need one hundred clients. If you are charging $2,500 a client, you need forty clients. By this calculation, you just reduced your workload by more than HALF. Talk about creating your dream life doing what you love. How good does that sound?

Now, the question is, how do you raise your fee without having the fear that no one will hire you, and feeling the guilt that you are overcharging?

There are a few ways to approach the process of raising your fees. To be clear, making sure you are choosing your ideal client also supports the understanding that you can charge what you are worth. When you believe in yourself and your ability to create and deliver a beautiful event for your client, you are able to set your prices at a level that matches your ability.

Raise your fee SLOWLY, but FREQUENTLY

Everyone has a set-point. A set-point is an invisible benchmark, comfort zone, target line, or whatever you want to call it. For instance, your set point for your weight is 150 pounds. One day, you step on the scale, and you see you are at 160 pounds, so you freak out and begin extreme dieting. Your mind and eyes are used to seeing 150 pounds. Gaining to 160 pounds crosses your set-point for your weight, so you want to get back to 150 pounds as soon as possible.

The same works for your fee. If you are used to charging $1,000, and you decide to increase your fee to $2,500, the next time you quote a client, you might have a very hard time verbalizing that new fee fluently and confidently. You may find yourself sounding a little unsure, timid, and even stutter when you name your fee. This is because the new number is so foreign to you that your inner voice is screaming, "What are you doing? That is not what we are used to charging, and we are going to lose this client!" This is because you are so used to saying, $1,000, and collecting $1,000, anything more or less than that will create an immediate reaction. That's the reason why we need to increase our fee slowly, so our body and mind don't go into shock. When the increase is small, the mind is able to adjust to the new number much quicker.

When raising fees slowly, you also want to increase your fee frequently. With small increments done on a frequent basis, your mind can be trained to see small increases over a short period of time. You will feel more comfortable quoting the new fee, because the increase is small enough that you don't choke when you say it. You are also able to align your belief in your self-worth to the new price at a pace you are comfortable with.

If you experience a scarcity mindset, do not transfer your head trash to your potential client! What I mean by that is if you think you are too expensive and start assuming your potential client can't afford to hire you, then you just convinced yourself that you are NOT WORTH the fee you are charging, or the potential client has the same scarcity mindset as you.

Do not assume anything. Remember how assume is spelled? You start to assume, and you make an ass out of u and me. If a potential client is talking to you, that means she is already seeing the value in hiring you. Why do you want to self-sabotage and assume they can't pay your fee, especially after you have qualified them during your sales process? This is discussed further in the next section.

If you do not charge your worth, you are ROBBING yourself. Do not feel guilty for charging your worth. This is a transaction. One must be willing to pay, and one must be willing to accept to make it a transaction. If you feel confident in charging the high fee and the client is happy to pay, take that money and do your job! If you feel guilty because you think that you are overcharging, then you are robbing yourself from making the money you deserve to make. If that's how you allow yourself to think, then stop complaining that you are not making enough money, and that people don't pay you for your worth. If this internal conflict sounds familiar, you need to start working on your mindset and how you value yourself and your work.

CLIENT BUDGETS

A potential client contacts you because they want to plan an event. What's the FIRST question that most event planners ask? I bet more than half of the event planners out there will ask, "What's your budget?" Unfortunately, several event planners fall into the trap of asking this question when they first meet their potential clients.

What Does Your Client Need Help With? This is not the place to start with potential clients or leads. You should never come out of the gate with this line of questioning. How could that be the first question to ask when you don't even know what the potential client requires you to do in order to determine if the budget is sufficient? Yes, they told you they need help planning their wedding, for example, but what do they need help with, exactly? If you don't know what they need from you, how will you know if the budget they share with you is realistic?

Qualify Your Lead

Converting leads into actual clients is pivotal in your business, without question. Before converting a lead, you must qualify that lead. The process of qualification involves assessing whether or not the lead actually does show promise for choosing your services. To begin, you must identify what is the problem your lead is trying to solve or what is the immediate need they are trying to fulfill. The second piece requires asking your lead what other resources, solutions, or ideas they have already tried to meet the need or solve the problem/challenge.

The last piece revolves around time and urgency. You will need to ask your lead if the challenge is one for which they will need an immediate fix or is this a challenge that can wait. One example is a couple who is planning a wedding who are looking for a wedding venue with a rapidly approaching date. They may have asked friends, family, Google, and they may have done their own searching, with no results. This is a good lead. You will also want to make sure to ask this lead how they found you.

Once they have found you, they will go through a process of a buyer belief hierarchy. Every time a client talks to you, they have several things going through their heads. Clients come to you with a problem, you give them a solution, and you describe ways you have solved the problem for others in the past and what you think you can do for them.

Your client will then begin to think about whether or not they like your solution. Then, they might begin to think about whether or not they can implement this solution on their own, for themselves. If they decide they can do it themselves AND have the time to do it themselves, then they won't need you, but if they decide they want the solution but do not know how to create it on their own, then they will most likely hire you to do it for them, as you originally proposed.

The psychology of this sale reveals a multi-layered process. In this whole process, your job as the event planner is to share with them your vision and your experience. You have to share with them what would be the experience like if they were to work with you, for example, when they work with you, they will save time, they will save money because you know how to negotiate a good contract and because you know how to look for venues through your preferred vendor and venue site lists. Most important of all, your potential clients should be enjoying the whole process of planning for their event. If you are the right event planner for them, you will have taken away the potential stress involved in orchestrating all of the moving parts and pieces. You will have shown them that life is going to be so much better if they hire you to do it for them.

Once you qualify the lead, and you have concluded that this lead is indeed your ideal client, then you can start talking about money. The "trick" here is ALWAYS talk about the money before you really talk about the money, which is when you name your fee.

Guide Your Client

The reality is how do you know if the potential client is telling you the truth when they share their budget with you? Sometimes (and often), they have no idea how much things cost (that's why they are talking to you). That's when we run into the "champagne taste, beer budget," situation.

Even though you don't lead with the question about your client's budget, you will eventually ask. It is imperative for event planners to find out what a client's budget is for the event before we can agree to plan the event, otherwise, you and the potential client will not be able to agree on ANYTHING because, again, the potential client has unrealistic expectations based on how much they want to spend.

Ultimately, it is our responsibility as event planners to educate and guide our potential clients when planning their events. We need to be able to bring these potential clients back down to earth by sharing what things actually cost to make their dream event a reality. Having said that, we never want to make the potential client feel "small" or "inadequate" or downright humiliated. "What's your budget?" is a sensitive question and one of the main reasons potential clients feel reluctant to share with you their "real" numbers because they don't want to be judged as being "cheap" or have their ego hurt.

ALTERNATE WAYS TO DISCUSS "BUDGET"

There are several ways to go about asking the budget question without getting into the tap-dancing routine or offending anyone. Here are a few tips.

Have you looked at any venues to have this event? If your potential client is looking at venues where you know the venue charges a high room rental fee or food and beverage minimum, then you know the client has a champagne budget. Don't be afraid to ask the potential client if they know how much the venue charges for rental fees and food and beverage minimum. This provides a great opener to the discussion of budget.

How many guests do you plan to have at the event? The more people they plan to invite, it's logical to assume that the host will budget more to feed these guests.

Can you share photos of how you want the event to look? Encourage your potential client to share with you their vision of what they want their event to look like. When you go over the images with them, ask them what items in the photos they like. Then you can politely ask them if they know how much those items (the items they pointed out to you) cost.

Is this a repeat event? If yes, where was it held last time? If this is a repeat event, you want to find out how much they budgeted for the last event and how much they ended up spending. That will give you a ballpark figure of how much they will budget for this year's event

If the party is at the host(ess)'s home, find out where (city, zip code) the house is located. If the house is located in a high-income area, that also indicates that your potential client may have high earning power.

Who are the people who are coming to this event? If you are planning a corporate event, you want to be very specific about this. If the people who are coming are top executives and C-level executives, the event will need to have a healthy budget, because this group of people are well-travelled, have discerning taste, and are used to the finer things in life.

HANDLING PRICE OBJECTIONS

Ah... the Price Objection. The P-word that we all roll our eyes at when we hear it from our potential clients. Our brain immediately goes into combat mode to get ready to tear down this objection by justifying why we are worth our fee and why these people need to work with us. I know your ego is hurt and you are thinking, "Why would these people think my fee is too high? Don't they know I provide top-notch service?"

Many times, the price may not be the main reason people don't buy from you. It is definitely one of the most convenient excuses to use without having to go into the real reason why they do not want to buy from you.

Take in a deep breath, my friend. Ego kills all deals, so instead of fretting and fuming, let me share with you the steps that will help you overcome price objections.

Step #1: Breathe and Control Your Emotions

You don't want to appear condescending, angry, or whatever beast you turn into when someone says

"NO" to you. It is natural to feel frustrated, annoyed, and even appalled when someone says no to your event planning services. You have so much pride in what you do and provide. You could not fathom how someone could possibly say "no." The next word that comes out from your mouth will very likely sound snarky without you even realizing it. The last thing you want is for a client to walk away because of the price AND bad customer service. So, breathe, and take a few moments.

Step #2: Ask Questions

After you have calmed yourself down, ask permission to ask questions to find out if the price is the real objection. The reason why we ask for permission to ask a question about the price objection is to move the client's emotions from defensive to neutral. For example, "You mentioned that you don't have the budget for it/the fee is too high. May I ask you a question about that? If budget is not an issue, will you work with me?" You want to isolate the objection until you find the real objection.

Step #3: Give Feedback and Build Rapport

If the price objection is real, give feedback by mirroring back what the potential client said to you. For example, "So if I am understanding you correctly, you want to work with me, but you do not have the budget. Is that correct?" If they share why they don't have the budget, such as they lost their job, or any other extenuating circumstance, empathize with them, and also, COMPLIMENT them for being careful with their money. Ask more questions and build rapport. They want to feel heard and not just feel us brushing away their objection and giving them our sales pitch again.

Step #4: Ask Questions to Vision Cast

We want to ask the TWO MOST IMPORTANT questions that would require the potential client to imagine two outcomes:

"What do you think would be the result if you choose to work with us?"

"What do you think would be the result if you decide not to work with us?"

The price is only a concern when the potential client cannot convince or justify to themselves that the results they are going to get are worth the fee you are charging. You want your potential client to come to these two conclusions:

1. The result they get from working with you far surpasses the cost of investing in you.

2. The result of not working with you will cost her much more financially, emotionally, physically, and mentally compared to the cost of investing in you.

Then you want to ask the closing question: "Based on those two outcomes, does it make more sense for you that we should work together?" By now, your potential client would have already overcome the price objection by themselves.

AHA! Moments

- When it comes to Business Finances, you must take care of your business first. Before you can take your earnings, you have to pay what you owe in labor, technology, marketing, etc.

- You only need a business partner if there is something you are not skilled at or passionate about and an employee or contractor can't fulfill that responsibility.

- Only negotiate with a vendor if you see yourself becoming a long-term partner with them.

- Do not undersell yourself. Provide what your clients need and they will be willing to pay it.

CHAPTER 6

WHAT YOU NEED & WHAT YOU DON'T NEED TO START YOUR EVENTS BUSINESS

There are lots of people out there who will offer advice on how you should run your business, even when they are NOT a business owner or have shown a track record of owning a successful business! It can be overwhelming and begins to sound like a lot of noise when you are just beginning, even if you are an established business owner looking to level up. To own and run a six-figure eventrepreneur business, you have to get very, very clear on what you need and what you don't, for yourself and for your business.

WHAT YOU NEED

1. First and foremost, you need a business plan. But more importantly, AFTER you create the business plan and set the stage for your business's success,

you need to show up for yourself. Yes, we need to show up for our clients and for the commitments we make through our business; however, the first commitment you need to make when undertaking a project of the nature that will ensure your six-figure income, commit to yourself the time, energy, and appropriate boundaries around what it is going to take.

When laying the groundwork for your business, as a part of showing up for yourself, please, please avoid multi-tasking. Shut down your 1,000 open tabs on your browser and be present with whatever task is immediately in front of you for building your business. If you can, put away your phone. If your phone is how you are accessing your materials, use the "Do Not Disturb," feature to protect your time and attention while working.

Avoid distractions. Stay committed to your work, while it is happening. Make the promise to yourself to hold yourself accountable and use the tools you have to allow someone else to hold you accountable, if needed. Find the support you need for that, which leads to number 2.

2. Good, reputable information. As a successful event-repreneur, it frustrates me that so many of you out there with the dream of also being successful event planners are given wrong or bad information around how to achieve your dream. Seek out great mentors to help provide you with support and valid, accurate, and helpful information that you need. Learn from

someone who has results to show like the ones you want to see in your own business.

Be very careful and selective about who you follow in the events and business field and then do your homework around those people. Check them out. Make sure they are who you think they are. We already know that a successful eventrepreneur is someone who turns their passion for events into a profitable business and follows the guidance of someone who came before them for support.

Keep in mind, you must be able to APPLY the great information you receive because you are compensated for what you do, not necessarily what you know.

3. The ability to act on the information you receive. Depending on who you ask, sometimes the advice you receive might be marginal. However, sometimes we receive GREAT advice, but we don't follow up on what is suggested or do anything with the information we gather.

If this is the case for you, I would encourage you to ask yourself why. Why have you not used the great information given to you? Or, if you used the information, are you happy with the results? Why or why not? Maybe, it wasn't great information for you, and in that case, okay. However, if you can honestly say that you have received great advice in the past regarding business building but haven't done anything with it, you must be self-reflective enough to examine why, and then self-correct.

This relates to your mindset and your ability to assess it regularly. Your current thinking provides your current results. In a growth mindset, self-audit becomes imperative to continuing to level-up your business and your personal life in concert with your Why.

4. Declare what you want to yourself and to people who believe in you and your dreams and abilities. If you don't declare it, claim it, and make it known, then the Universe does not know what you want or how to help bring it to you. Be proud and declare that you want to be an Unstoppable Eventrepreneur ™. Wear that title with pride.

5. Listen to how you talk to yourself and how you allow others to talk to you. I can teach you all the techniques and tactics; you can learn from YouTube, online courses, other coaches, whoever, but if you don't control your mind, your feelings, and your emotions, which are your most powerful tools, it won't stick. Have you heard the saying "your thoughts control your actions; your actions produce your results?" If you are talking negatively to yourself, you will NOT take inspired actions, and the results will not be the results you desire.

As mentioned previously, your mindset is of supreme importance to your success, and part of working on building your business requires that you keep a constant check on your mindset. You will have to be able to train your mind; without this skill, you will be weak.

There are lots of challenging questions and situations that you may encounter, and you must be able to answer these challenges with wisdom, calm, and poise as a reflection of your mindset. We all have the tendency sometimes to talk ourselves out of something or into a corner, to come up with all the reasons why something isn't possible. Stop your "no's," and start asking, "What can I do now?" This touches on the Employee mindset vs. the CEO mindset discussed in Chapter Nine.

6. Don't ever apologize for your accomplishments or for your ambition to be successful. There was a time when I did not allow myself to relish my accomplishments or feel good about what I had done, based on my previous relationships with money. Allow yourself to celebrate your wins. It is important to continue to allow them in your life! If you do well, stand up proudly and own it.

7. Good relationships with your vendors. Finding the right vendors who align with your vision and your brand. Collaborating with your vendors is key to keeping a low overhead and not getting bogged down with inventory you don't need and cannot store.

8. If you want to build a business, you need to know your numbers. You need to track your revenue and your expenses. My guidance, away from owning office or venue space and away from needing your own inventory, is based on steering you away from having a high overhead. If you are looking to be a six-figure eventrepreneur, a solvent business owner,

you MUST have a handle on your financial health and your bottom line's ability to handle risk.

9. Experience. You have to have a solid foundation in the event planning business. If you don't know how to do something, you learn how. One of the best ways to do this is to shadow someone. You can volunteer or join a mentorship program. Grab an internship. You can take courses, read blogs, and watch YouTube tutorials (I have all of these available).

   However, you can, get experience with or learn from a great event planner. On the web, mayyeosilvers.com is a great resource. Knowing how to plan an event is not going to make you money—that's a hobby. If you really want to make money in your business, you need to learn how to turn your hobby into a profitable business.

10. Marketing materials. One important question I receive on this point revolves around whether you have to have all of this in place before you launch your events business. I suggest having a website created, your social media accounts set up, and your business cards (digital and/or hard copy) always available. For website creation, however, let me give you a few things to consider here.

    Keep your language simple and direct for clarity in reaching your ideal client... the simpler, the better.

    When building a web site, the three-second rule applies: you need to capture attention within three seconds. Your website visitor should know within 3 seconds what services do you provide, who do you help, how do I work with you, and why should I work with you? Make your answers to these questions very bright and bold, with consideration for SEO (search engine optimization, tag words). There are several free services to help you do this, in addition, there are websites that contain free images for you to use.

Be aware of your font size, no smaller than 16. Your contact button should be on every page, if possible. Put yourself in the shoes of your potential clients, considering who is your ideal client. Make sure you have great testimonials from your friends and clients in order to showcase your talents and to help illustrate your worth!

The reality is you never stop marketing yourself. Do you have to have ALL of your marketing materials in place before you market yourself? No, you complete these processes concurrently. If you know how to create excitement and inspire your potential client, they will still want to work with you, even if your marketing materials are under construction.

Rule number one in my mentorship program: You always shamelessly market yourself. You are always putting yourself out there and making people aware of what you are doing in your business. Rule number two is to refer to rule number one. If you have zero visibility, you have zero business.

11. Business Plan. Very often, people do not create business plans. At one time, I did not even have a business plan for my event planning business, M2 Hospitality. When I found myself in a tough situation,

I had to create one. My second business, Events4Anyone has an intact, working business plan that I work with and shift regularly, as needed.

Don't overcomplicate it. You are not writing a journal or a thesis, and this is not necessarily a document that you will take to the bank to ask for money. Just make sure you address the what, why, who, where, and how. What services do you want to provide, why it is important to provide those services, who will want and need your services, where do we find these people, and how you can communicate what you can do for them.

I have shared with you all that you need to start your six-figure event planning company as an Unstoppable Eventrepreneur, so how much money do you think you will need to create your business? Create a budget for yourself, across your life, to be able to afford to pay for the support you will need whether it is business cards or a website builder. Stop eating out once a week to save the extra money, if you need it. When there is a problem, there is always a solution. Don't limit yourself by thinking you don't have choices and resources. You do. It is up to you to decide if you want to adopt the solutions available to you.

If you are talking negatively to yourself about not being able to afford something, but you do not want to sacrifice a meal out or a latte to be able to have the extra cash flow, that is a decision you have made. You can't lament not being able to afford a website if there is an available solution that you simply don't want to accept.

The law of polarity holds that if you say "yes," to something, you are also saying "no," to something. Don't complicate things. Mistakes are going to happen; you learn from your mistakes. If mistakes happen, at least you know you are doing something. This far beats sitting in a corner, waiting to act from a fear of failure or of wanting to do everything perfectly. How is something going to be perfect if you are not out there practicing your craft and implementing what you learn?

Business is like being an athlete—you practice, you learn, you audit, you get better, you practice, you learn, you audit, you get better. The only way to learn something is to just go and do it.

Your business plan will need to account for your Why, your synergy, and your area of passion. It should account for your mission. This is how you will execute your synergy.

Your vision will also need to be included, and this is how you see your company growing and changing, regarding your mission in regular increments of time. What kind of services will you offer to achieve your mission, and how much do you want to sell them for? Who will buy these services? Think about where you want your business to be at the end of six months, one year, two years, and even five years. This helps you create your financial projections. Your business plan will help you craft your marketing strategies. From there, you can create your timeline and build your financial target goals around that timeline.

If this is your side hustle, I suggest having six months of savings accounted for in your business plan to be able to pay your bills, if needed. As you grow and evolve, are you consistently selling enough to have these savings? Do you have work in the pipeline at all times that allows for you to have six months of savings? If yes, then you know you are approaching the position of being able to quit your other job and dedicate your time to your event planning business as your main income stream.

A part-time CEO will spend an average of forty to eighty hours per month on business building; a full-time CEO will spend more on the order of 160 hours per month. Be realistic when you make your projections. This piece also relates to your risk appetite, and this topic is covered in Chapter Five.

As a part of the business plan, you will need to understand how you want to structure your business. You never want to structure your business as a sole proprietorship. You want to structure it as an LLC, because it detaches you and your personal assets from the business. In other words, if there was ever an issue and someone sued you, as an LLC, they could only access your business assets. Whereas, in a sole proprietorship, you and your personal assets could also be legally attached to the lawsuit.

If you have a business partner, though I don't personally recommend or advise it, you will need to have an operating agreement so that roles and duties are accounted for and agreed to ahead of time. Everyone needs to pull their weight.

12. Insurance. In time, you will need to make sure you have business insurance. When you start charging money for your services, it is advisable to purchase general liability insurance and professional liability insurance. General liability insurance protects you, your employees, and your contractors. Professional liability insurances protect you based on the fact that you are dispensing advice in a professional capacity.

WHAT YOU DON'T NEED

1. One obstacle I often hear from event planners that hinders from starting their events business involves the idea that they don't have enough money to rent an office space, or that they don't already have an office space available.

   I am nine years (while writing this book) into a multi-six-figure business, and I don't have an external office space, outside of my home. Why? As an event planner, we go to our clients, they don't come to us. We meet our clients in their homes, office, a café, or at event spaces in order to be able to tour and assess whether the space will work for their purposes. Why would we need to spend the extra money on an office, when it will be frequently empty? I am based in Miami, but my events are all over the country and STILL, if I want to take a month vacation to Singapore where I am from, I can do that and work from there.

2. The second thing you don't need regards your mindset, again, and how you talk to yourself. I can't say it enough: Stop with "I don't know…," or "I don't have…" You don't need the negative self-talk and getting a handle on it by actively watching what you say to yourself (see previous list), helps to keep that in check.

3. Inventory… as in, decorations, audio-visual equipment, tablecloths, chairs, anything you can think of that might be a physical component or item as a part of a successful event.

   You don't have to have all of that! What is your title? Are you a rental company, or are you an event planner? Think of how quickly trends in decorating change. If you are trying to offer top quality events in trend, and you were to try to purchase and offer this, it would be financially unsustainable.

   Now, think about storage for all of these items, which will no doubt change throughout the years. How could you have enough room in your home and in your garage or attic for all of these things? Or, you end up with so many things that you have to rent a storage unit to contain them all? No, you don't need to approach the details of planning your events this way. Stop buying things! Now, some event planners have a system for this, and it can work for them. I just don't recommend it. You may be thinking that the client bought the inventory, and you get to keep it, so there's no cost. Well, when you are using the inventory to go set up and tear down for the next event, YOUR TIME IS COSTLY! It would cost you

EVEN MORE because the time you spend on the manual labor could be time spent on sales generating activities, like chatting with the host and guests so you can get leads for the next event!

You could have your clients buy the inventory and give it to them when the event is over. If they insist that you keep it, then resell that inventory! You can collaborate with other event planners who already have inventory, just don't ever spend your own money buying inventory for an event. This is where good relationships with your vendors helps you.

4. A venue space. As an event planner, you do not need to have a venue space to start your event planning business. If you are still working on figuring out how to build a client base, how will you know how to get clients to book your space? Now you NOT ONLY need to know how to get clients to book your event planning services, but you also need to know how to get the client to book the event at YOUR VENUE. Between staff, mortgage, insurance, and utilities, the cost for this kind of space is huge.

   Put the ego aside and realize that you don't need to be able to offer clients an event space to be an event planner. If it is your dream to own a venue, keep the dream alive; it will come true. However, you must prioritize earning a solid, steady, large income first, and that is why you have picked up this book.

5. You don't need any kind of certification to be successful. Your potential clients don't know any-thing about certifications as they are not from the events field. They also don't care if you are certified

or not if they don't jive with your personality or don't trust you to handle their events. If a certification of some kind makes you feel better, or gives you confidence, great. Make sure you are seeking certification from an internationally or nationally recognized organization whose credentials are solid and reputable.

People buy from someone who makes them feel they will be listened to and cared for. Theory is great, but of greater importance in owning your business is your ability to gain visibility, how to market yourself, how to get leads, how to convert those leads into paying clients and knowing your finances. Hands-on experience will do more for you toward this end than any kind of certification.

6. Finally, building business is a lifetime commitment. It is building a legacy. Don't be hard on yourself in the process, and still, hold yourself to your tasks in order to reach your goals.

AHA! Moments

- Avoid distractions when it comes to your business. You know what is best for your company, hold yourself accountable and responsible for it.

- A good mindset will bring positive results. Remember that you are the positive force that can bring good results.

- A sound business is built from a sound business plan. Don't over complicate it. Use it as your north star to guide your energy and your actions to yield the results you want.

- Know how to spend your money. You do not need elaborate decorations, a venue space, or a whole building. Spend what you know you need for your business.

- Remember your time is money!

CHAPTER 7

THE EMOTIONAL ROLLERCOASTER RIDE OF EVENTREPRENEURSHIP

With the exception of the last chapter of the book, the conclusion, this will be the shortest chapter. This is mostly because I don't want you to dedicate too much time to getting bogged down in being upset, worried, frustrated, angry, or sad. I don't want you spending too much time on any of the negative emotions that come up in our lives at different times, let alone the ones that happen when you are making a potentially scary leap of faith into the unknown by starting your own event planning business. Being an eventrepreneur implies courage and strength, but it also means being human, feeling, and addressing the hard feelings along with the happy ones.

Think about the following scenario: You start your business with enthusiasm, you think everyone is going to love you and love what you do. So, you might have started with more passion than planning. You have one or two clients, you are excited, but since there was no plan, there is no pipeline for further business when you have completed the work for your first few clients.

When the business doesn't just arrive on its own, you begin to wonder if perhaps your first few clients were a fluke. You start to doubt yourself. You run out of money. All of the questions start coming up, "Am I even capable of doing this?"

What is worse than not having business? When you have had business and the business goes away. You have momentum, and then the momentum stops. This leads you to take clients who low ball you in offering payment or ask for a discount. You start giving discounts, because you fear not having work or money. As this process progresses, without the proper business plan structure and mindset for focusing on your why and marketing yourself, you are drawn back into the security of a "job" that has you working for someone else again. There is nothing wrong with this...but there was a reason you wanted to work for yourself in the first place.

Breathe. Sit in a quiet place and realize that there are going to be moments on the journey to being a six-figure business owner that require you to see beyond JUST the moment you are experiencing. Just because you are experiencing difficult emotions or challenging situations in life or business does not mean that you have to give in to them or to resort to poor coping skills. Nor does it mean you have to give up on your dream.

I included this chapter for the purpose of being real with you. The path of an entrepreneur is not for everyone, but with your focus on your Why, your training, your desire, your passion for events, and the proper support along the way, it can be for YOU.

CHAPTER 8

FEAR AND COMPETITION

We recently did a poll inside our Facebook group asking our members if they are fearful or fearless when it comes to their event planning business. The results informed us that we have a lot of fearful eventrepreneurs, and also, a great number of fearless eventrepreneurs, which is encouraging!

How can you tell which one you are? There is no right or wrong answer to this question. It's not good to be fearful, and it's not good to be fearless either. I will explain why.

IF YOU ARE FEARFUL

If you belong to the fearful camp, I want you to ask yourself these three questions:

1. Did your fear arise from a past experience? If yes, why are you allowing your past to dictate your future?

2. Is your fear even real? Evaluate your present environment and opportunity. Is there data or

evidence that supports that whatever you are fearing is going to happen?

3. Are you in control of your fear? If no, why not?

I want to invite you to join me in this mental visualization exercise. For the fearful eventrepreneurs, I want you to imagine your fear (a.k.a., your inner critic, that devil that sits on your left shoulder) as a big bully. Put a face to that bully, someone that you couldn't care less about and have negative feelings towards. I want you to put a face to that big bully.

Then, I want you to visualize that bully kicking you and hurting you badly each time you decide to implement something for your business, be it raising your fee, trying a new marketing strategy, or trying to close a sale with a potential client. Each time you want to attempt something for your business, this big bad bully is kicking you at every angle, hurting you so badly that you could hardly stand up, so all you could do is curl up like a ball and let that bully kick you, berate you, tell you that you are worthless, that you are good for nothing, and there is no way you can succeed in anything you try to do.

How does that make you feel? Did you feel anything when I asked you to visualize that scenario? Can you literally feel the pain that the big bully is inflicting on you physically, mentally, and emotionally? If you felt nothing, that means you are so immune to the pain that your inner voice, the devil on your shoulder, that imaginary big bully has been inflicting on you that you have just accepted it as part of life.

Ask yourself, if, in real life, someone is abusing you the way the imaginary bully is abusing you, would you accept it as part of life? If your answer is no, then why would you allow your inner voice, a.k.a. the bully, to abuse you and cause you to make the wrong decision for your business?

If you did feel something when you played out the whole scenario, then I want you to ask yourself if you have ever done anything to fight that bully back. If your answer is yes, did you win? If your answer is no, you didn't win, then ask yourself if you got stronger each time you tried to fight it. The key here is you TRIED to fight it. Because the more you try, the stronger you become.

It is NOT normal to accept that type of emotional abuse that you allow your inner voice to inflict on you.

Overcoming Fear

Time to take a step back to create a common understanding of what constitutes fear. What exactly is fear? It has so many names. These may include insecurity, uncertainty, and low self-esteem, just to name a few. Is fear a learned behavior or are we born with it? Personally, I believe it is a learned behavior.

Look at a baby for instance. When they are learning how to walk, they are not afraid of falling or the pain that comes with falling. They fall, they get up, and they try again. They have no fear! As adults, we have so many fears. Fear of failure. Failure is a BIG word with so many different meanings. That word itself probably encompasses many, many fears.

If you remember all the way back to Chapter One, I describe my own experience with fear and the sheer will required to overcome it. These fears were not just simple, run-of-the-mill things that scared me. These fears belonged to me as a wife and mother looking to have financial solvency and the ability to pay my bills, even on my own if I had to do so.

I am lucky enough that I have a great support system, but I was also taught not to depend on anyone else for my financial health. It took strength, courage, and straight-up hustle to finally quit the jobs I had taken, hoping for financial security, which were actually distracting me and keeping me from growing my own business into one that could sustain me and my family in the long-term. I had to get very comfortable with my fears, in order to transform them.

A New Friend

This brings me to the strategy that worked for me, and it might just work for you too. What if we could turn fear into our new best friend? Does that sound crazy to you? Well, it sure did to me initially. I chose to befriend FEAR because I believe in keeping my friends close and my enemies closer, and FEAR is my enemy numero uno, so I started labeling it as *friend*. Just as when you decide to make a new friend, you want to know more about this friend, right? So, I decided to try and understand what the fear is. Once I understood more about the fear, then I was able to set out to find solutions to overcome it.

1. **Talk to people who have experienced the same fear.**

   Ask them why they feel/felt that way, and how they overcame that fear, if they did. If they didn't, you could brainstorm together about ways to address the fear you both share. Once you find people who are going through the same feelings as you, you know you are not alone, and fear becomes less threatening and scary.

2. **Dissect the fear.**

   Analyze the pros and cons of letting fear take over. Is it more fearful to do something about the fear, or should I just accept the fear and live with it? Which is more painful: Staying fearful or looking fear in the face and telling it that you are its new BFF, that you are not afraid of what it threatens any longer? If your path is to befriend the fear, come up with an action plan to tackle the fear. You need to show your new "friend" who's in charge here. That might mean giving it a seat at the table, simply to keep your eye on it.

3. **What can you learn from fear?**

   If you had an experience that you would associate with a specific fear, ask yourself, what you learned from that experience? Why was it so fearful? Acknowledging the fear gives you clarity on why you felt it so intensely that it keeps showing up. Once you understand where the origin of the fear is, often you will realize that the fear is unfounded and frankly, downright silly.

As an entrepreneur, and even in life, if you are not experiencing some form of fear or being uncomfortable, then you are stagnant in personal growth and in income growth. I am not saying that we shouldn't stop and smell the roses. I am saying we should deliberately expose ourselves to some form of "fear." The more you do it, the more your brain gets used to the feeling of being fearful, and being able to sit with it, without feeling the need to run from it or chase it away. Eventually, the feeling of being fearful gets smaller and smaller.

In my world, fear means new challenges, which in turn means growth. Remember, the most dangerous place to be, especially in business, is to be "comfortable." Getting comfortable with being uncomfortable can expand your capacity in life and in business.

IF YOU ARE FEARLESS

If you belong to the fearless camp, I want you to ask yourself this question:

When you decide to try on a new marketing strategy for your business, do you do your background work to find out if this new strategy is suitable for your business and your target audience, or do you just dive in blindly?

Now, let's try another mental exercise. This time, I want you to imagine yourself as this fearless warrior going to fight a war. You are fearless, so you go out charging towards the enemy line without any plan of attack, armor, and no backup.

What do you think will happen to you? The answer is obvious. You will get hit, injured, and probably get killed! A warrior who is not prepared before going to war is not fearless, he is plain foolish and reckless.

Apply that to your event planning business. I applaud you for taking imperfect actions, but every imperfect action has some form of behind-the-scenes prep work, so your imperfect actions can yield some results.

Do Your Research

If you decide to try new strategies to grow your business, but you didn't do any groundwork to get the necessary information to decide if these strategies are aligned with your brand, the services you want to offer, or appeal to your target audience, then you will be "killed" when you go to market. You get "killed" because you just wasted your hard-earned money and wasted precious time and resources without getting all your facts right. It's great to take risks for your business, but it has to be a calculated risk.

I do want to caution you to NOT fall into the camp of "analysis paralysis" because you want the decision to be a calculated risk. Just know that you will never be able to get ALL the data you need to make a calculated risk decision, but as long as you have done your preliminary research and trust your gut, then you can be fearless when presented a business growth opportunity.

Moving forward, I want you to turn fear into fascination. Fear is basically the "unknown." If you allow yourself to be fascinated by the unknown instead of being paralyzed by fear, then you will open yourself up to possibilities of knowing how to conquer the unknown. You will start to look for resources to "arm" yourself, so you are ready to fight that big bully, and go to the fight prepared as a fearless warrior. This relates directly to your mindset, discussed in Chapter Three.

COMPETITION IS GOOD

Mindset also affects how you approach competition, which is inevitable in any business. When I hear someone say, "There's too much competition. I can't get into that business," I cringe.

Listen, if there are not a lot of people or businesses offering the same product or services, that means there is no demand for that product or service. Do you want to get into a business where there is not enough demand to support what your business offers? That is business decision suicide move number one. The more demand for a service or product, the more businesses or people that will supply that service or product to meet that demand, hence, competition! This also means there are people out there who want and need what you are offering.

So, how does that apply to event planners? How are you going to stand out in this saturated market (says you)? Let me share some nuggets of wisdom on what I think about competition and how you can squash competition and kick it to the curb.

1. Competition Is NOT REAL!

Unless you have a clone that you are not aware of, the only competition is YOU! You and many other event planners may offer the same type of event planning services, but they are NOT you. You have your own way of presenting yourself and your services. More importantly, people buy from people whom they trust and like. So, your personality, values, morals, and beliefs will attract your ideal clients who like you for who you are because they are a version of you.

Remember: Not everyone is your client, and you are not everyone's planner.

2. Not Everyone Plays the Same Long Game

If you want to be in a category of one, you need to start thinking like a category of one and train like a category of one. Many business owners, not just event planners, go into business thinking they can make a lot of money working very few hours to grow their business. If you are willing to go the extra mile and put in the extra effort CONSISTENTLY, you will be in a category of one. No one can touch you.

3. Stop Comparing the Worst of Yourself to the Best of Others

You have no idea how the best event planners out there started when they first had their businesses. They might have been as insecure, ignorant, and inexperienced as you. Don't compare your day one to their day one hundred! The only person you should be comparing to yourself is... YOU! Start comparing your past to the present. Look at how much you have progressed professionally and personally. Constantly assess how you can do better in order to define your category of one.

To me, no competition means no growth. No growth means, "You are dead to me," quoting Mr. Wonderful from Shark Tank.

A word of advice: If you keep looking back to see who is behind you (your competition), your eyes are not looking forward to seeing where you are heading. Stay focused, look ahead, and share your brilliance with the world!

AHA! Moments

- Fear is not always a bad thing. Let it motivate you to do better.

- If you don't have competition, something is wrong! Competition ensures that there is a demand for your services.

- Don't fall into the overthinking camp. This is what we called "in limbo." You are not really fearful because you are thinking to take a calculated risk. But you are also not fearless because you are overanalyzing everything because you are fearful of making a mistake. Gather the NECESSARY data, trust your gut and move forward!

CHAPTER 9

MINDSET OF AN UNSTOPPABLE EVENTREPRENEUR

As we have established, leaving behind fear and competition takes courage and commitment to the work in front of you. As an Unstoppable Eventrepreneur, you will have many things demanding your attention, and your ability to keep things going in the right direction and on track with your business plan is part of what makes you a fantastic event planner!

Being realistic, things might not always go as you have planned them to go. Hopefully, more often than not, they will, but I want to talk about the fact that it's not always what you do when things are going smooth that makes you successful; it's what you do when you are down that determines your grit, your resilience, and challenges your WHY to propel you to the next level. Consistently showing up, even for the rough days, will propel your business forward.

Something to think about: if you are engaged in communities with fellow business owners for networking, support, and potential business building ideas, it can seem that others are further along in the process than you are, and it can sometimes cause you to feel like maybe you are behind the curve or not doing something you should be. It's okay, keep heart. There will always be business owners, fellow eventrepreneurs who are farther along in their journey than you are: this does not mean you are doing something wrong or that you aren't doing something you should be!

Your journey to six-figures is your journey; their journey to six-figures is their journey. Each business goes at its own pace, just as each person goes at their own pace. You are the only one who can evaluate and hold yourself accountable to what you "should" be doing for your business. Mentorship and community are valuable tools to help provide and share information about what works and what doesn't; however, you are the CEO of your life and your business, no one else.

This chapter will help you build the mindset (discussed in Chapter Four) for building your successful event planning company, with the understanding that you drive the direction, the momentum, and the capacity of your business.

UNDERSTANDING YOUR HABITS

Your mindset, how you view yourself and the world, is greatly affected by what you choose to give your attention to each day. This includes your daily routines and habits.

How you have been programmed in the past, to just try to survive under pressure or in chaos, is not how you want to continue. You want to break that habit because it is not healthy or "normal." If you keep going back to the way you have always done things, what you have always been doing is going to continue to give you the results you have always been getting. Nothing will change. If you want your business to grow, you need to grow first. Your strategy or tactics will only take you so far… If your mind doesn't grow, your business won't grow.

For example, pick a work habit that you have, good or bad. What has that habit produced in your life? Is the result one you want to keep, or do you want more from yourself? I am going to suggest a journal exercise using the following language: "My habit is_____. I have done this for a long time, what it cost me is _____."

I will use an example from my own life to illustrate.

"I had the *habit of not talking about my feelings*. I did this for a long time. What it cost me was *passive-aggressiveness, anger, and frustration*. I was angry all the time."

Do you have any behaviors in your life that need to be examined and shifted? Using this process of self-evaluation to identify and address habits and activities that no longer benefit you, helps you to grow personally, and allows that increased capacity to be put to better use in your personal life and in your business. Pull back and assess if you are working in the best way possible right now, if you aren't, you can shift it and change it. If you don't know, you need more conversation around this topic. I am always going to send you back to try and tap into Why you wanted to start your business in the first place. It creates the foundation for everything you are doing.

Some people may not understand why they need to understand their Why! Going back to your Why will help you do the deep work that needs to be done when you are making the push to level up your life and your business. This is what I am asking you to do, for yourself. I can give you all the information in the world, but ultimately, it is up to you to determine the trajectory of your life, and therefore, your business. Make sure the habits you cultivate support your Why. There is always room for improvement.

When creating and scaling your business, there must be a transition that takes place at some point in the process. Most of us have worked for others throughout our life. We have been great employees in working for others, showing up each day, and doing what is expected of us. Our schedules have been created by an entity outside of ourselves.

The transition takes place when we take full responsibility for our time, creating a schedule with intention that reflects what we hold to be most important to the achievement of our goals. We become our own boss. Even if our event planning business is still a side-hustle, we prioritize realizing our dreams, by letting our daily activities and habits support the realization of the dream. We shift from working for someone else to working for ourselves, thereby becoming not only CEO of our business, but of our entire life. We achieve the alignment discussed in a previous chapter.

EMPLOYEE MINDSET VS. CEO MINDSET

There are a few things to discuss at the outset regarding the transition from being an employee, working for someone else, and making the leap to be your own boss. There are a few common pitfalls that affect many eventrepreneurs when transitioning our business from a side hustle to the main event or when your business begins to hit its stride. Growth requires expansion.

I have outlined the 3 distinct differences between an Employee Mindset vs an Unstoppable Eventrepreneur CEO mindset

1. Security

An employee perceived a regular pay check as security. An unstoppable eventrepreneur understands that true form of security is created BY you, not given TO you

As CEO of your events business, you need to learn to perceive the unknown as a opportunity instead of a potential failure

2. Initiative

An employee is an order taker. An unstoppable eventrepreneur is a problem solver.

An employee expects to be given instructions and resources on how to handle a task or challenge. An unstoppable eventrepreneur will do their own research for instructions and resources to handle a task or challenge. They are action takers, they don't want for things to happen, they make things happen.

3. **Accountability**

An employee gets the opportunity to not have to take accountability if something doesn't go right. "This is above my pay grade." is the common excuse.

As an unstoppable eventrepreneur, the buck stops with you. You must hold yourself accountable for your actions AND your lack of actions. Your business is driven by you. Do NOT blame environment, other people, or life. It's either you control life or life will control you.

Because of this, you must be organized. If you cannot bring order and organization to your life and your business, you will burn out, and you will burn out quickly. If you are tired or exhausted every time you execute an event, something is not right. Listen to the cues your body, mind, and spirit are giving you.

CEO SCHEDULE

Here you are… in the thick of it. You are actively engaging in the pursuit of the dream of your six-figure eventrepreneur business. Your CEO schedule is vital.

Your CEO schedule includes your daily life. It isn't all about business. Not only are you the CEO of your business, but you are the CEO of your whole life.

Fact: Maintaining a CEO perspective affects your personal life as well your business life. This is a topic I am often approached with by my mentorship clients, the challenge of work-life balance and the CEO schedule.

As event planners, most of us face this challenge. The answer lies in being intentional with how you spend your time. Speaking plainly, living hour-by-hour and day-by-day without an intentional plan cannot support a six-figure business. If you are looking to start your event-planning business, and you just can't seem to find the time, or you feel so overwhelmed with your full-time job plus the demands of your family life, this can prevent you from making the required leap of faith to begin.

If you feel that anytime you set out to accomplish a task, you end up getting derailed or pulled off-task to fulfill someone else's needs, I am speaking to you. There is a better way that will allow you to meet your family's needs as well as your own!

Three Principles for Intentional Planning of Your Daily CEO Schedule:

1. Place EQUAL importance to both your business schedule and personal schedule, especially if you are building a new business. Many of us will put our existing schedule first, as it currently flows, then work on the new business in any free time. Instead of fitting your new business schedule into your current schedule, you need to fit your current schedule into your new business schedule in order to be able to grow. If you are just starting your business and are still employed full-time somewhere else, your personal life and current work schedule contain very important tasks that must be done, but your dream job as an eventrepreneur and six-figure business owner also has very important things that need attention.

In order to begin evaluating how you spend your time to flip your schedule, first, you need to figure out what are the non-negotiable items in your personal life. This includes your mental, emotional, physical, and spiritual health, as well as your family time. Then, you must determine what are non-negotiable items for your full-time job, the main one being that you must show up for work. Finally, you must determine what are the daily, non-negotiable items required for growing and scaling your business. Creating sales, creating visibility, engaging on your social media, engaging with others on their social media, reaching out to past clients, reaching out to past leads, responding to current clients and potential clients. All of these client-facing duties must be on your schedule. Business non-negotiables include the items that are going to push your success needle faster.

Once you have identified the non-negotiables in each area of your life, I want you to have a second look at them. Run them through the filter of your Zone of Genius, a.k.a., what YOU are best at doing. Ask yourself again, "Are all of these items truly non-negotiable?" Once you have your answers and necessary tasks clearly in front of you, you can then decide what you are able to automate, delegate, or delete.

Focus your CEO energy on the items in your Zone of Genius and create a plan for the rest of it. For example, you can automate your social media posts using different apps or software that allow you to schedule posts in advance. Delegation means you ask someone else to complete the task for you. My example involves me asking my husband to pick up our daughter from school and transport her to different activities if I have a particularly busy day.

Sometimes I can't do it all myself, and so I ask for help, or delegate that non-negotiable. I ask for help, and I encourage you to do the same thing. You do not need to be Superwoman; ask for help. Deleting something speaks for itself. Sometimes, you just have to cut something out, and that is okay, but there needs to be balance among the non-negotiables in your life to keep yourself healthy and happy and to allow you to do the work you love to do.

2. You must make your CEO schedule as though you are already running a successful business. For example, if you do not currently have any clients, you might be inclined to do something else with the time you would use reaching out to them. Instead, continue to prioritize that time and keep it on your schedule, whatever the business task may be, because when your business starts to pick up and you DO need all the time you can get to complete them, you will be less likely to be scrambling to find the time if you have allotted the time for those prioritized tasks from the beginning. There will always be something you can do to grow your business during that time so the allotted time for the activity that does not currently exist would never go to "waste."

Be very mindful of prioritizing your allotted business time because what happens when you end up growing. If we are scrambling for time, we often tend to then take away from our personal time in order to get work done. This can lead to confusion, exhaustion, and overwhelm—the very things your CEO schedule is designed to help you avoid.

3. Respect your own schedule and respect the boundaries that must be in place for you to complete all the tasks for which you have blocked your time. If you aren't going to protect your schedule from distractions, what is the point of making a schedule in the first place? If something keeps happening to distract you from what you have put on your schedule, perhaps that distraction is actually something that needs to be put on your schedule and given attention. This is not always the case with distractions, but it can be. However, if those distractions are not non-negotiables, then respect the schedule.

Also, make sure that people around you are respectful of your schedule, as well. I spoke previously about how the people you share your life with must be on board with you as you go about building and growing your business. They don't necessarily have to support you, but they cannot be what hinders you either. They need to respect what you are doing, even if they don't always like it.

Involve your family and your team in creating your CEO schedule. I do this with my husband and our daughter as well as the people I work with. They know I work out in the morning. I also do my self-learning during this time. I do not take any calls before 10:00 a.m. because that is my CEO schedule, which allows me to take care of myself first. I do not take any client calls on the weekend either because that time is allotted for my family.

So, no one feels like they are being robbed of time, I politely explain to any potential clients that this is part of how I plan my life, and that means respecting the schedule I have created for myself and the people I love. If you find that your partner, your children, your mother-in-law, your family in general do not respect your schedule, it is because you don't respect your schedule enough to set and stick to a boundary.

Often you will have to help them understand why they need to either wait until you are available, or they can have someone else meet their needs, if they need immediate attention. This can also take practice. If you don't respect your own CEO schedule, how can you expect anyone else to respect it?

If you make a CEO schedule and it is not working, think about the idea that you may be creating it in an unrealistic way. Maybe you are trying to cram too many things into the schedule in one day. Another possibility if you find your schedule dysfunctional, perhaps what you have included is not actually what you really want to be doing in the first place, even though you have allotted time for it.

Therefore, you allow the distraction to come in; if you know that the distraction being presented is not a non-negotiable and is not going to move your business in the right direction toward six-figure success, why would you entertain the distraction? The only conclusion can be that what you say you want in your personal and business life is not actually that important to you. If it is, you need to tell that distraction, "I can't help you right now, or I can't help you at all." If you allow a distraction, then understand, you are accountable for it.

Also understand that your business growth can be hindered if you allow too many of these distractions to take you away from your CEO schedule. Take accountability and understand the consequences of this dynamic for your business and for your personal life. Every action that you take, every decision you make, is going to have some kind of an impact. Therefore, you MUST be intentional with your time. You must be able to accept the consequences of all the choices you make for yourself and for your business in this regard. No one can take accountability for the trajectory of your business based on your CEO schedule and how well you organize your time. Your choices are yours and yours alone when it comes to this.

Finally, your CEO schedule is not just a one-time creation. It evolves and changes as your business grows and changes. The first time I did my CEO schedule, it took me five hours to create! You will always tweak your schedule to make it work the best for you, your personal life, and your business life. It is constant evolution and improvement.

Taking responsibility for your CEO schedule helps you recognize, own, and stay in your power as you grow into the six-figure business owner you are destined to become. Stay mindful and present with yourself and what you are looking to create; stay mindful and present with your Why. It will help drive everything you do, every choice you make.

THE BIG DIP

Which basically means suddenly your business loses momentum and no sales are coming in, what do you do?

First of all, understand that this is to be expected. Nothing is permanent. No business goes up all the time, and no business takes a nosedive all the time.

When you hit the BIG DIP, you need to evaluate what were the actions/lack of actions that caused the dip? You then implement the solutions. Understand that you WILL always be able to crawl up from a big dip. In business, it is not ONLY what you are doing right that gets you growing, but also what you are doing when you are DOWN. For example, how many times you get up and how fast you get up will both also catapult you to the category of one.

AHA! Moments

- You are not like everyone else, so why would your eventrepreneur journey be the same? There will always be someone ahead of you and that's okay.

- Understanding your habits and why you have them will help you grow and break the bad ones.

- You must stay organized. Maintain a balanced work and personal life and respect the boundaries you set for yourself.

- Just because business is slowing down, doesn't mean it's ending. Look back at why it's slowing and make a plan to fix it.

CHAPTER 10

CONCLUSION AND STANDING BY YOU

When I asked myself why I wanted to start a business coaching program for event planners, my first thought was that I have been blessed with people in my life who had helped me to get to where I am today: An owner of two successful events-related businesses. I am able to wake up every day doing what I absolutely love—planning events and mentoring event planners.

I want to be able to "pay it forward" by inspiring other event planners to truly honor their passion for planning events and build a lucrative business from that. I want to be the same people who helped me when I was building my businesses.

I want to be the role model, and the "right cat to copy" by offering tried and true methods, practical, actionable, and sustainable ways to grow a business. I want to cut through all the noise and BS (at least in my opinion), of what other people are saying in the market on how to build an event planning business. That's the main reason why I put the 10 Rookie Mistakes at the beginning of this book, to debunk all that "advice" given by these so-called experts in the events field.

You can learn as many things in as many different ways as you want to, but if you don't apply courage and blind faith to implement what you have learned, then nothing will come to fruition. Before we even talk about implementation, let's focus on mindset. If you don't do the deep work of being acutely aware of how your current mindset is dictating the decisions you make/don't make, the actions you take/don't take, then you most likely will not be able to interpret or understand why you are where you are now instead of where you want to be.

I understand business, and I understand the nature of human beings. My superpower is the ability to understand the blocks that my clients have that are hindering them from taking actions and creating the life they truly desire to live. I have put in a lot of hard work over the years, did major inner work on my mindset, and taken actions to expand myself and my businesses. When I present what I know and what I have learned, it is from a place of deep caring and a deep desire to help you create the life you want for yourself.

You have chosen to achieve this dream through the pursuit of your passion for event planning and a strong commitment to your Why. Will this process be easy? No, but it will be worth all the effort you are making. You are worth that; your loved ones are worth that.

In closing, I want to leave you with one thought: you don't have to do this by yourself. I am available online through multiple platforms. All those handles are listed below.

Reach out anytime. Learn more about my Unstoppable Eventrepreneur Mentorship Program™ to work with me and my team directly.

website: www.mayyeosilvers.com

LinkedIn: www.linkedin.com/in/mayyeosilvers

Facebook: www.facebook.com/mayyeosilvers

Facebook private group:
https://www.facebook.com/groups/events4anyone

IG: www.instagram.com/mayyeosilvers

TikTok: https://www.tiktok.com/@mayyeosilvers

Podcast: *The Unstoppable Eventrepreneur™*

ABOUT THE AUTHOR

May Yeo Silvers is an event planner and business coach with over 20 years of experience in event planning, hospitality, and entrepreneurship. She is the founder of M2 Hospitality and Events4Anyone, the host of the podcast *The Unstoppable Eventrepreneur™* and the author of the book *The Unstoppable EVENTrepreneur™*

As a happy wife, proud mom and successful event-repreneur, May's journey began in her home country of

Singapore where she took on a position as a food and beverage trainee at the Raffles Hotel, Singapore. It was there that she fell in love with the hospitality industry and decided to pursue a career in the field.

After being in the hospitality field for 7 years, May decided to take a sabbatical and became a senior sales executive for a sports management company. It was there that she learned to cut her teeth on sales, cold calling, and negotiation. After being one of the top sales person in the company, her passion for the hospitality and events field brought her to Miami, Florida in 2004 where she helped to establish the events and food and beverage departments at The Setai, a brand new luxury hotel overlooking the iconic South Beach.

May eventually worked her way up to Director of Catering and Conference Services and Director of Event Planning at several luxury hotels, including the JW Marriott Marquis Miami and The Royal Palm, South Beach, where she was part of the hotel's opening team.

In 2012, May left the hospitality field and created her own event planning company, M2 Hospitality where she worked with well-known corporate clients in the banking and legal fields. May married her previous experience as an insider in the hospitality industry with her sales and negotiation skills to ensure that all parties mutually benefit from the contracts negotiated and built a lasting business relationship.

Today, May continues to plan events and focus on creating events that are financially beneficial, deepen relationships and build brands, while ensuring guests feel valued and well taken care of.

May's unique approach to building her event planning business (no inventory, no expensive overhead), and her entrepreneurial spirit, led her to start Events4Anyone, a coaching company designed to help event planners start and grow their event planning businesses. May is passionate about helping her coaching clients understand the ins and outs of the event planning industry, while giving them the mindset shifts and the no-nonsense support they need to turn their passion into profits.

Like what you have read? If you'd like to work with May, scan the QR code to find out more about the Unstoppable Eventrepreneur Mentorship Program™.

For more great books from Peak Press
Visit Books.GracePointPublishing.com

If you enjoyed reading *The Unstoppable EVENTrepreneur*™, and purchased it through an online retailer, please return to the site and write a review to help others find the book.

www.ingramcontent.com/pod-product-compliance
Ingram Content Group UK Ltd.
Pitfield, Milton Keynes, MK11 3LW, UK
UKHW020620030225
4412UKWH00006B/96